CONVERSATIONS
ON *Customer Service & Sales*

INSIGHT PUBLISHING
SEVIERVILLE, TENNESSEE

CONVERSATIONS
ON *Customer Service*
& Sales

© 2005 by Insight Publishing Company.

All rights reserved. No part of this book may be reproduced in any form or by any means without prior written permission from the publisher except for brief quotations embodied in critical essay, article, or review. These articles and/or reviews must state the correct title and contributing author of this book by name.

Published by Insight Publishing Company
P.O. Box 4189
Sevierville, Tennessee 37864

10 9 8 7 6 5 4 3 2

Printed in Canada

ISBN: 1-932863-26-5

Table Of Contents

A Message From The Publisher

Some of my most rewarding experiences in business, and for that matter in my personal life, have been at meetings, conventions, or gatherings after the formal events have concluded. Inevitably, small groups of ten to fifteen men and women gather together to rehash the happenings of the day and to exchange war stories, recently heard jokes, or the latest gossip from their industry. It is in these informal gatherings where some of the best lessons can be learned.

Usually, in informal groups of professionals, there are those who clearly have lived through more battles and learned more lessons than the others. These are the men and women who are really getting the job done and everyone around the room knows it. When they comment on the topic of the moment, they don't just spout the latest hot theory or trend, and they don't ramble on and on without a relevant point. These battle scarred warriors have lessons to share that everyone senses are just a little more real, more relevant, and therefore worthy of more attention.

These are the kind of people we have recruited to offer their insights and expertise for *Conversations On Customer Service & Sales.* The book is filled with frank and insightful discussions with men and women who truly understand what it means to succeed in the arena of selling, and then servicing their customers! It is ripe with "the good stuff," as an old friend of mine used to always say. Inside these pages you'll find ideas, insights, strategies, and philosophies that are working with real people, in real companies, and under real circumstances.

It is our hope that you keep this book with you until you've dog-eared every chapter and made so many notes in the margins that you have trouble seeing the original words on the pages. There is treasure here. Enjoy digging!

Interviews conducted by:

David E. Wright
President, International Speakers Network

Chapter 1

JOHN ERIC JACOBSEN

THE INTERVIEW

David E. Wright (Wright)
Today we are talking to John Eric Jacobsen. John is the founder and president of Jacobsen Business Programs in New Jersey; a training and seminar company whose mission is *"To provide innovative information in a motivational and entertaining format, enabling his clients to enhance the quality of their business and personal lives."* John is an award winning, dynamic motivational speaker, and much sought-after trainer with a very unique and diverse background including twenty years in business management, training, consulting, theatrical arts, and hypnotherapy. Some of John's top-of-the-line clients include: The United States Army, United Defense, The United States Department of Chemical Defense, Subaru of America, and many more. John Jacobsen, welcome to *Conversations on Customer Service.*

John Eric Jacobsen (Jacobsen)
Hi, David! I'm honored to be on your program.

Wright

John, you have an amazing client list and you're a very successful entrepreneur. In your two decades of presenting corporate training, what are some of the most important things you've learned about customer service?

Jacobsen

David, believe it or not, I'm not a very big fan towards the idea of customer service. I believe the philosophy is truly important, yet the concept is old, tarnished, and worn-out. Today's marketplace is super competitive, and a business cannot survive on good customer service alone. Today, good customer service is not enough! In order to achieve the pinnacle of success and stay ahead of the pack, Corporate America needs to shift its thinking away from customer service, and magnify its focus on creating euphoric and loyal relationships with their customers. Good customer service should be a byproduct of the loyal, strong relationships you have created with the people who support your business—not the other way around. Personally, I enjoy receiving good customer service, yet the businesses that I consistently prosper are the ones who treat me like I'm family. I feel very strongly about this.

Wright

Those are very powerful statements! Can you give us an example?

Jacobsen

Sure! A simple one comes to mind: There are three dry cleaning establishments in my community. All three are reliable and provide excellent customer service. However, only one of them has earned my business—and kept it. Their name is "Crispin Cleaners."

On my first visit to this particular establishment, I had my one-year-old daughter, Erica with me. The very personable ladies behind the counter insisted that they take a small Polaroid picture of her and hang it on their wall for all of their customers to see. Being a very proud and flattered dad, I happily agreed. One week later, my daughter's picture was hanging on their wall for all to see. This simple act touched me so deeply that I have been sending them referrals and business ever since. Today, they have dozens of other family's pictures hanging on their walls. I estimate that I have spent over $5000.00 at this establishment over the years. That's quite a return on their money considering the original Polaroid probably cost them less than 10 cents. Of course, they provide excellent customer service, yet their attention to my daughter turned me into a loyal and faithful customer. Also, I know this example will not be applicable to every type of business. The point to remember is to build relationships.

Wright

I agree with you! Tell me, what are some ways we can begin to build these relationships with our clients?

Jacobsen

In my Customer Service Seminars, the first strategy I teach to all the CSRs is a philosophy I keep alive in my own business. And that is "to treat all of your customers as if they were your mother or father, sister or brother, son or daughter." And more importantly, you must do this sincerely. It must not sound like lip-service—you must truly mean it. People are very smart, and if you are phony or insincere, they will see right through you and your sale and client will be lost forever. Ask yourself honestly, "Would I sell this product to my mother?" Or, "How would I like my spouse to be treated if they were in this business/customer relationship?" This mindset is critical if your goal is to keep your customer for a lifetime. Believe me, the moment you fumble a customer, someone else will quickly recover them.

Wright

Would it be a good idea to invite all of our clients over for every Holiday dinner?

Jacobsen

(Laughing) Only if you really feel compelled to do so. However, you do want to treat them in such a manner that they subconsciously believe that they would be welcomed.

Wright

What is the best way our readers can begin to incorporate your ideas successfully in their own businesses?

Jacobsen

Training! First, all heads of business must realize that all of their employees are "internal customers." Presidents, CEOs, managers and supervisors must be thoroughly trained to treat their employees (internal customers) exactly as they wish their external customers to be

3

treated. The manner in which you treat your employees is the same treatment your employees will deliver to your customers. We must strive to improve our managers' awareness of and ability to be a role model for service. Top execs must lead by example.

I'll tell you something else that interests and disturbs me, David. Lately, I've been noticing that many people in upper management positions are too busy to attend training sessions or seminars. Instead, they send middle-management or the front-line staff. Their job is to then report back what they have learned. I understand that an overwhelming schedule and overbearing workload can restrict your time. However, the world is changing at such an expeditious pace, that only the lifelong learners will be able stay in the lead on the corporate expressway.

That being said; after the training is satisfactorily completed, then upper management must commit to training the entire company on the most valuable ideas learned. These ideas must be put into a "Best Practices List" and distributed to all employees. In order to build trust and credibility, it's crucial that every employee is trained to treat each customer with respect, courtesy, and honor. This exceptional revere will give your company what I like to call the "mark of distinction." This is a wonderful characteristic to have and something that your competition will envy.

Wright

You mentioned training. What type of training do you recommend?

Jacobsen

Well, certainly not customer service training. That would be my second or third recommendation. My suggestions to any CSR or sales rep are courses on "Interpersonal Skills" and "Business Etiquette." These may be the most important courses of your career. Highly developed people skills are essential. These are truly your most valuable and lucrative corporate assets. I believe people skills are more important than technical skills. I'll tell you something else, David. With over twenty years of experience in this business, the most successful sales people and CSRs I have ever dealt with all had consummate people skills and those skills served them very well.

I travel an extra ten minutes down the road whenever I need gas because the employees at that particular station treat me as if I'm family. There are other filling stations closer to my home, but they were never friendly. They never smiled or said hello. They rarely looked at me or said thank you when taking my money. Needless to say, I happily took my business elsewhere.

You know, David, there's an old expression, "Treat your customers like gold." Of course, I disagree with that one. My belief is to treat them better than gold. Treat them like family. And why? Simply put: Our customers do more for us financially than our families do.

You know, David, I have a wonderful family. They are the greatest family in the world. However, my family doesn't pay my mortgage or my electric bills. My family doesn't put gas in my car. My family doesn't buy my clothes or pay my daughter's school bills. Tell me, David, who do you think pays all of my bills?

Wright

Your customers and clients.

Jacobsen

That's correct! My customers pay all of my bills and allow me to lead the kind of life I do. And to thank them, I will constantly strive to treat them with loyalty and respect, and give them the best service humanly possible. And the best way to accomplish this is to polish and perfect your people skills.

Mr. Anthony Gigante is a dear friend of mine and a very success-ful entrepreneur. He recently told me that his rise to the top of the sales ladder was sometimes very difficult. However, the friends and relationships he created years ago during his climb are the same peo-ple keeping him at the top of his game today. He taught me that interpersonal skills and customer service need to be synonymous. This is a very valuable lesson that I share in all of my classes.

Wright

So, John, the message you're sharing with us today is that making the sale and making a customer happy are not enough. How can we know when we truly served our customer well? How do we know if we are on the right road to creating loyal customers?

Jacobsen

I hear that question a lot. And there are four measuring posts that will let you know you are doing a great job. They are four questions you must ask yourself after every customer interaction:

1. After the interaction, did your customer or client feel better about themselves because they had met you? Did they feel as if they'd made a friend?
2. Did you exceed your customers' expectations?
3. After the interaction, did your customer feel as if they had made a good business decision or have their problem completely resolved?
4. Is your customer sending you referrals?

Believe me, David, if you can answer "yes" to those questions after each client encounter, you'll be in the top 10% of highest paid sales people or CSRs in our country. The sincere relationships you build with your clients will prosper you beyond your grandest expectations.

Wright

I have never heard those questions put across in that manner. Can you expand on them and tell us why you believe they are important?

Jacobsen

David, I believe question # 1 is the most important of all. Question # 1 is a measurement as to whether or not you have built your client's self-esteem. And building the self-esteem is the greatest emotional gift you can give to any human being. By building a client's self-esteem, they begin to associate you as a "source" or "font" which allows them to feel better about themselves. These emotions create a tremendous amount of rapport, trust and credibility, leading to a lifetime of loyal customer relations. If you re-read the questions, they are a simple common sense approach to building human relations. And as we've been discussing, human relations should always precede customer service. Obviously, question # 4 is an indication of how well you've done your job.

Let me give you some ideas about how to successfully execute steps 1 and 2. Firstly, helping your customers feel better about themselves and exceeding their expectations is done by fully understanding and continuously furnishing your customers with the mandatory "Six Basic Needs."

The first and the most basic of these needs is **friendliness.** A friendly persona and atmosphere are an integral part in creating loyalty. You can create a friendly atmosphere by greeting clients warmly at the door or over the telephone. Your handshake must be professional and inviting. You should be happy to see or meet them, smile and use gentle eye-contact. During your conversation give them a sincere, specific compliment about something you may have noticed. Remember, if this is your initial meeting or first contact with the customer, the first impression you give can make or break the deal.

The first three to five minutes of your interaction should be in exchanging pleasantries. This is another great way to build rapport. The rest of the meeting should revolve around business, sales or problem solving. When the interaction is over, conclude with another professional handshake and thank them. I know these sound like common sense, and they are! However, my observations lead me to believe that in many sales and customer service interactions, common sense is not all that common. We must strive to get back to the basics and then consistently apply the basics with everyone we encounter.

Wright

I agree! Sometimes we can get so caught up in all that's new or flashy that we forget about the basic foundations that support our business. Continue please.

Jacobsen

You're so right! We need to get back to the basics, and relationships need to be the cornerstone. For example, David, did you know some research indicates that it takes less than fifteen seconds for your customer to get a "first impression" of you.

Wright

Yes, I'd heard. Imagine that! You have just fifteen seconds to persuade a new client to do business with you. It's almost as if they are carrying around an imaginary report card and are mentally scoring everything they like or dislike about you.

Jacobsen

Well put! In just fifteen seconds your customer will notice your personal hygiene, how well dressed you are, if you are wearing too much perfume or cologne, if you're excessive in your jewelry, if your clothes are clean and pressed, all the way down to if your shoes are polished. I realize this sounds harsh, but your client is making all of these judgments about you in order to determine whether or not you're someone they'd like to do business with. This is why the friendship quotient is so important. I can remember in my early career trying to sell a package of seminars to a Fortune 500 company. Apparently I went a little overboard with my cologne because the lady interviewing me had a severe allergic reaction to it. Needless to say I lost that deal. Today, I look back at that unfortunate memory and I can laugh. But the day it happened I was devastated and very humbled. Much earlier in my career I had a client tell me that I had the weakest handshake he'd ever experienced. He said something to me that I'll remember the rest of my life. Are you ready for this one, David?

Wright

Yes, I am.

Jacobsen

He said that I could never be truly successful unless I knew how to shake hands. He also said that my handshake is more important than my resume. Once again I was devastated and humbled. It was not until that day that I realized how much your handshake can reveal about you. People do not want to do business with someone who does not know how to shake properly. After that I attended a mini-course on "handshaking etiquette" at the local college. Sorry, David, I did not mean to go off on a tangent about handshaking. I just firmly believe it can make or break a business relationship.

Wright

No, No! It's very interesting. Can you give us some handshaking tips based on what you learned in that mini-course?

Jacobsen

Well, the first thing we need to remember is that it's called a "handshake," not a "finger shake." Never shake someone's fingers! Make sure you take their entire hand in yours. Then give a firm, polite grip. There is no need to squeeze as if you are a vice, and it's not necessary to break bones. Shake only two or three times as you smile and give gentle eye contact. Then, smoothly, let go. It's that simple.

Wright

Simple, but many times overlooked. You've mentioned "gentle eye-contact" twice already. What does that mean?

Jacobsen

Gentle eye-contact means that you must never stare into someone's eyes as if you are insane. That type of eye-contact is incorrect and can cause an instant breach in rapport. Remember if it's a gentle gaze—it's eye-contact; if you're staring-- it's stalking. Your eye-contact must always be gentle, kind, non-threatening and friendly.

Speaking of friendly, let's get back to that basic need. As sales people and CSRs we have to remember that people love their names. By constantly remembering and using your client's name you are demonstrating an enormous amount of respect. Another idea is to call them for no reason, or just to say, "Hello." Try to remember special things about their family or friends. Remembering birthdays, anniversaries, and special events can be a tremendous way to build loyalty and trust, especially if you can send them a card. If your company is having a special event, invite your customers. I recently opened a bank account at a new branch in our neighborhood. They threw a huge picnic for members of the community in order to generate interest in their banking services. Hundreds of families attended. There was free food and drinks, clowns, and balloons for the kids, music and so on. It was a huge hit and they generated a lot of business.

The second basic customer need is of **understanding and empathy.** All our customers need to feel that their positions and feelings are respected and fully understood by us without judgment or criticism. Mr. Angelo Salandra, another dear friend of mine, is the founder and President of the very successful Quality Copy in Philadelphia. While vacationing recently, he received a frantic phone call from a client who needed twenty-five sets of 405 originals to settle a very important court case. The copies had to be collated, bound and delivered to the courthouse within six hours. Mr. Salandra cut his vacation short, successfully completed the job, and personally delivered the job to the courthouse. His client was truly grateful and appreciative. In this particular instance, I believe he went beyond the call of duty in demonstrating his understanding and empathy for his client's dilemma. And it worked! He became a valued client for over seven years.

The third basic customer need is to feel as if they have been **treated fairly.** This need is usually high on everyone's list.

Wright
It's high on mine!

Jacobsen

Mine, too! Recently, I was waiting in line at the Motor Vehicle Department to have my picture taken for my license. In a moment of my not paying attention, a large gentleman cut in front of me on the line. Before I could say, "excuse me," the agent behind the counter shouted at the gentleman, "He's next—not you!" The rude line-cutter humbly stepped aside and let me go first.

Wright

Wow! That must have made you feel special and justified.

Jacobsen

It did, especially because I had waited on the line for twenty minutes prior. I felt as if I was treated fairly and that my time was respected.

The fourth basic need is to feel a **sense of control**. All people like to feel as if they have an impact on the way things turn out. Over the summer, I needed my sprinkler system repaired. When I phoned in for a service call, the CSR allowed me to pick the time and day I'd like the system to be repaired. This choice gave me a tremendous feeling of power and control. It also allowed me to choose a time that was convenient for me so that I did not have to rearrange my hectic schedule. I also decided to do business with that repair company from that day on. That type of courtesy and convenience is priceless.

The fifth basic need is that of **options and alternatives.** All customers like to know that there are other avenues available to help them get what they want if necessary. Alternatives are also another way of giving a client control. Simple things such as: Various shipping or delivery methods, different models with variations on price, flexible store hours, acceptance of different forms of payment, and product guarantees are ways in which you can make it easier for your customer to do business with you. In my seminars I teach that the more you convenience your customer the greater their loyalty and patronage. I believe the art of convenience can create a reputation of excellence for your company.

Finally, the sixth basic need is **information.** Our clients need to be educated and informed about our policies, procedures and products. Brochures, booklets, flyers, and of course, websites are very valuable in these instances.

Wright

I love the idea about the six basic needs. What about the third question or measuring post? What are some things we can do to resolve customer issues and help them feel that doing business with us was a good choice?

Jacobsen

There are many answers to that question, David. First, we must accept complete responsibility for our errors and admit mistakes. If possible we should admit our mistakes before our customer brings them to our attention. Although lately it seems some corporate conglomerates have forgotten, "Honesty is **still** the best policy."

As a friend to your customer, you must be accountable in all that you do. Accountability is a sure sign to your customer that they are dealing with a legitimate company, and can help you build rapport. In many cases rapport with your client can be so deep that they over look errors and easily forgive mistakes. This is what family and friends do for each other, and another vital reason for building loyalty. Always deliver when promised if not sooner, and be prompt with your return calls or e-mails. These are basic courtesies that many businesses seem to have lost sight of.

Today most of our customers talk to automated machines, not live people. I realize that this saves time, but for the frenzied customer it may not be an option at that moment. To remedy this, your outgoing voice message should always state an approximate time they can expect a call back. Then be sure to return the call as promised.

Here are a few more ideas that have been helpful for me when resolving customer issues:

1. Use your body language and voice to indicate your sincere willingness to help and resolve the problem or issue.
2. Use your body language and voice to demonstrate your high level of self-confidence and patience.
3. Smile when appropriate and keep an open posture. This can help lower your customer's defenses leading to a speedier resolution. Remember your main goal is to build rapport-- not resistance.
4. Listen fully and take notes if appropriate.
5. Use silence often and never interrupt. Remember a closed mouth gathers no feet.
6. When speaking use an even, conversational tone.

7. Avoid company jargon. This can cause your customer to feel isolated or out of the loop.
8. Use appropriate humor when required. I am a firm believer that if used properly, humor can move mountains.
9. Try to make an optimistic statement whenever possible. This can help the customer see a light at the end of the tunnel.

Most importantly show your clients how much you value their opinion by constantly asking for feedback. Remember, David, good service is in the eye of the beholder. Your measurement of quality service might not be what your customer believes it to be. So by asking for feedback you can clearly meet your customer's needs each time, every time.

In my seminars, I teach the CSRs and sales reps to view all feedback as a "gift." When your customer gives you feedback or criticism, they are literally giving you a recipe for how they want you to serve them. It is also an unconscious clue that they are willing to do business with you again if you make the required changes. One of the surest marks of good character is our ability to accept personal criticism without feeling malice to the one who gives it. So thank your client for all of their feedback, then take this "gift in disguise" and run with it.

Wright

I agree with you totally. We should see criticism as a gift from our customer. That is very profound!

Jacobsen

Criticism should always leave us feeling as if we've been helped. So when we view feedback as a gift we can be saved by criticism instead of ruined by praise.

Wright

What about the irate customer? In some instances, despite your best efforts, the customer may be very dissatisfied and simply want to complain, scream and vent. What suggestions do you have in that case?

Jacobsen

First of all if they are screaming try to take them to a place where other customers cannot hear what's happening. That situation can create a larger unnecessary disturbance. Once you have the customer in a private area let them vent and complain as much as they want, and do not interrupt them. It's important to remember, David, sometimes people just want to be heard. They need someone to listen to them. Although it may not always be pleasant, as a CSR that is our job. While they are venting I always recommend that you imagine they are a loved one or a very special friend. Again, this simple mind shift can help you stay calm in a highly charged situation.

Be professional and empathetic. In other words, put yourself in their shoes. However, do not allow yourself to get drawn into their anger and begin to take their negativity personally. The manner in which to do this is to remain detached from their personality and keep all of your focus on the issue and solution. The more you focus on your angry customer's personality, the more likely it will be for you to lose your cool. The greater your focus on a positive outcome the less likely you are to be distracted by negativity. In some situations it may be helpful to take notes. This strategy will cause the customer to slow down their angry, fast paced ranting, so that you can catch up with your much slower note taking. Then finally, when it's your turn to speak, soften your voice and speak in an even, conversational tone. Keeping your voice at a low volume can cause the person to calm down faster, giving you greater control. Once the problem is resolved it is crucial that you offer a sincere apology. Apologizing demonstrates your deep "understanding and empathy" referring back to the six basic needs. A professional apology usually consists of 5 steps:

1. Sincerely say, "I'm sorry."
2. Sincerely ask for forgiveness.
3. Assure your client that you will take every measure to prevent the problem from occurring again.
4. (If necessary) Ask the client if you can somehow make it up to them.
5. After a few days, send them a note to apologize again or give a follow up phone call.

Step 5 is a very valuable tool to build rapport and honorability. Many businesses feel it to be unnecessary, however; I believe it to be an imperative extra step toward building momentous human relations.

Wright

John, what about if the customer is wrong? In other words, while dealing with a disgruntled customer you both realize that the mistake or blunder was the customer's fault from the very beginning. How can we respond in that situation?

Jacobsen

I've been there many times and I must repeat what I've been saying all along. Regardless of where the responsibility lies, treat them as you would your mother or father, brother or sister, son or daughter. This is the focal point of all human relations. This will give you the mark of distinction and your client will remain loyal to you and your company.

However, back to your question. As a good CSR, your only response must be to "save their face." Do not rub their noses in it. You will not score any points by proving your customer wrong or by making them feel dim-witted. Instead, go out of your way to make them look good regardless. Saying things such as, "It could happen to anyone." Or, "I've made the same mistake many times," can be a real rapport builder. The words you choose in a situation such as this can destroy or repair a client's perception of who you are. So choose your words and how you convey them very carefully.

Your words can also help you make a deep emotional connection with your customer and further ignite the six basic needs. I always recommend that all of my students keep a copy of the six basic needs very close by. In this manner, you can refer to them in the heat of the moment and create a safe environment for your client. Since your customer is the reason you have a job, you'll want to avoid squabbling or bickering with them. Remember, your job is not to win fights, but to win loyal friends. Our customers might not always be right, but they are always our customers.

Wright

John, there may come a time when we need to deliver bad news to a customer. What are some of your ideas on this?

Jacobsen

Sometimes my brother Mark and I co-teach our customer service training. He was asked the same question in a recent seminar and he gave several great suggestions. First, look for an alternative. If you promised your customer a certain product that is no longer in stock, give them an upgrade at no charge. In many cases, a comparable or upgraded product will quickly ease our clients' disappointment. An airline recently bumped me from a flight home. I was very angry because I felt it was a terrible inconvenience. In order to resolve the issue and turn me into a happy customer, they booked me on the next flight, put me in a first class seat, and gave me a free round-trip ticket to a destination of my choice. This was much more than I ever expected. I was still disappointed with the delay, but very happy with the compensation.

If no alternative is available, then you must notify the customer as soon as possible. Your notification must get to the point quickly and always be done in person or over the phone—never by letter. This is a positive step in treating your customer fairly and demonstrating your recognition of their value. Finally give a sincere apology, and ask for a second chance in the future.

Wright

What about "Thank You Notes?" Are you a fan of those? Do you recommend them?

Jacobsen

Not only do I recommend them, I believe they should be an integral part of every business if they are used properly.

Wright

What do you mean?

Jacobsen

In order to get the greatest impact from your thank you note, it must be sent out within two days of the sale or interaction. I believe your note should be handwritten to give it a more personalized feel. If your penmanship is less than desirable, type the letter or purchase a thank you card. And most of all, your note must never contain any ulterior motives. In other words, after your word of thanks, don't ask them for referrals, or try to sell them something else. I see these inappropriate actions many times, and I feel it's a big slap in your client's face. Simply express your sincere appreciation, say thank you, and mail it. It's that simple, yet very effective.

Wright

John, I'm aware that your company teaches a very popular stress management program. Do you have any special survival techniques to share with us as we go back into the trenches?

Jacobsen

As you know, David, keeping up a positive attitude all day long can be a very overwhelming task. Yet, despite the stress and pressures that come with the job, you cannot become a service super-star unless you are able to consistently maintain that positive mind-set.

So, here are some tips: Every day before you head out to work, spend two or three minutes visualizing exactly the way you want your day to turn out. By giving your brain a mental blueprint of what you expect from the day, you greatly increase your chances of having it turn out the way you imagined. I am a very big fan of visualization. I use it very often and very successfully. I always skip the morning news. Most of it is negative and that negativity can distort your thinking and cloud your judgment. I like to practice healthy thinking, therefore, I do not cloud my mind with negatives.

Pay close attention to your self-talk. The little inner voice that speaks to you all day long can have a tremendous impact on your productivity. So keep your internal dialogue positive by constantly affirming that a great day is ahead. Use affirmations such as: "I'm doing my best work," or "Today will be my best day ever," and so on.

Challenge yourself to find something interesting about everyone whom you meet, and try to learn something new from each of them so that you can share it with colleagues or your family.

Try to avoid any negative people that you work with. Stay clear of the complainers and criticizers. These people can cause you to drown in an ocean of negativity. Instead get to know someone with a great attitude and try to model them. Remember your attitude determines your altitude.

I also recommend keeping pictures of your loved ones on your desk or work area. Looking at pictures of your beautiful children or of a best friend can really change your mood from negative to positive. It can also turn a boring work environment into one that has a taste of home. Take your normal breaks and thoroughly enjoy them. Reading a positive book, listening to uplifting music, or simply taking a walk can be a great de-stressor. And most of all you must train your mind to focus on all of your successes. Make a list of your great accomplishments and the things you are truly grateful for and review them often. Carry the list with you. Read it in the morning, before bed, before a sales call or after a difficult appointment.

Finally, try to remember that dealing with the general public can sometimes be very challenging. It's very difficult to be a sales person or CSR, and we are very special people to be able to perform as we do. It's a constant battle to focus on what the customer thinks, feels and wants. However, we must strive to always put the customer first. Our goal is to be consistent, upbeat, accommodating, friendly, and provide service with and from the heart. This is true measure of value and human relations at its finest.

Wright

Well, this has been a terrific conversation. I certainly learned a lot and feel very motivated. John, I appreciate your time and want to thank you for your enthusiasm.

Jacobsen

David, it was an honor, and I look forward to speaking with you again.

About the Author

John Eric Jacobsen has been conducting professional human skills programs since 1984. He has developed proven techniques and strategies helping people to succeed in both their personal and professional lives. For more than two decades, John has excelled in motivating, coaching, instructing, consulting and hypnotherapy; training over half a million individuals to accomplish positive changes in both behavior and attitude.

Some of John's specialized programs include: Stress Management for Professionals, Interpersonal Communication Skills, Dealing with Difficult People, Emotional Control in the Workplace, Surviving Change, Conflict Resolution, and many more.

CLIENTS INCLUDE: The United States Army, The United States Marines, The United States Department of Chemical Defense, Interlake Steamship, Pepsi Cola, Alcon Surgical Laboratories, Subaru of America, Comcast Cellular, Corning Inc., AT&T, Warner Lambert, United Defense, GPU Energy, West Virginia University and Norwest Mortgage.

ON-SITE SEMINARS: Are our specialty! We can customize any seminar or training to fit your organization's needs. And we can present it to your group (whether it's 10 or 500 people) at a time and location that's convenient for you. Our goal and mission is to provide information, education and training that enables people to improve the quality of their lives and enhance professional productivity.

THE BOTTOM LINE: When it comes to helping people reach new levels of personal and professional achievement, nothing is more effective than Jacobsen Business Programs, Inc.

John Eric Jacobsen

Jacobsen Business Programs, Inc.

Marlton, New Jersey 08053

Phone: 856.988.7266

Email: JJacobsen343880@comcast.net

www.JacobsenPrograms.com

Chapter 2

THE INTERVIEW

David E. Wright (Wright)

Today we are talking to Brian Tracy. Brian is one of America's leading authorities on the development of human potential and personal effectiveness. He is a dynamic and entertaining speaker with a wonderful ability to inform and inspire audiences towards peak performance in higher levels of achievement. He addresses more than four hundred thousand men and women each on the subject of personal and professional development including the Executives and staff of IBM, Arthur Anderson, McDonnell Douglas, and The Million Dollar Round Table. His exciting talks in seminars on leadership, sales management, and personal effectiveness bring about immediate changes and long-term results. Brian has a bachelors in communication with a master's degree, and is a chairman of Brian Tracy International, a human resource company based in San Diego, California, with affiliates throughout America and in 31 countries worldwide. Brian Tracy, thank you for being with us today on *Conversations on Customer Service and Sales*.

Brian Tracy (Tracy)

It's a pleasure, David. Thank you.

19

Wright

Brian, trainers have changed sales format several times down through the years. It seems that recently relationship selling is recommended as the most successful format. Do these changes represent advances in techniques?

Tracy

Well, selling has really never changed. They've done fifty-five thousand interviews with customers to find out the process that they go through to buy, and there's a specific process that the customer goes through that the salesperson must dovetail their presentation and their interaction with. First of all, the customer has to like the person and trust the person they are talking to. So on that basis, relationships are very important. If I don't like you, I won't buy what you're selling, no matter how good the price is. So therefore, you have to have some kind of a relationship because the most important word in selling, I believe, is the word "credibility," which means that your claim is believable. And since human beings are primarily emotional, if I like you, I believe you more. If I dislike you or I'm neutral toward you, I'm far more skeptical or suspicious of what you say. So relationships are essential. Just the same as dating or going out with another person, the person has to like you a little bit in order to go out with you on a date. With regard to selling, the process is always the same.

First of all, the customer decides that you're a likeable and trustworthy person. Then the customer is open to talking to you. The customers only enters the sale when they realize that they have a need, and up until the time that you ask them the right questions and uncover the problems, and suggest perhaps that they could be better off in a cost effective way, customers are usually not interested, or at least detached, distanced, skeptical, unsure, uncertain, and so on. It's only when you touch on a need that the customer has, and the customer realizes, "Aah, I have that need. I didn't realize it before." Only then do they become interested because needs are what trigger interest. In nature it would actually trigger emotions, and only then do they become interested in finding out how that need can be satisfied in a cost effect way. It's something that really never changes. It starts off with the relationship. It goes to the identification of the correct need. It goes to the presentation of your product or service as a solution to that need, and then answers the question and closes the sale.

Wright

Yeah, that sounds a lot like when I first started several years ago, the sales process was divided into three parts, or at least the training that I had. The formation gathering phase, the presentation phase, and the close. Does that format still work?

Tracy

Yeah, we sometimes say that today you have to be a doctor of selling. A doctor does three phases. First of all, they do a thorough examination. Second of all, they do a diagnosis based on the examination. And third, they offer a prescription and encourage you to take it. In our live sales seminars, where we have thousands of people, we say the three keys are to prospect, which is to find people who can buy and can benefit from what you are selling; to present and show them that what you are selling makes sense to them in a cost effective way; and then it's to follow up and close, which is to get them to take action. So it never changes. It's still the same three in order.

Wright

I've noticed that down through the years in my selling, the close has—I don't define it as I used to. Close was something where I ask for the order, and there was a closing presentation, and all like that. I find that now people buy from me without really having to close.

Tracy

The reason for that is the more thoroughly you diagnose a person's needs, and the more clearly you explain that your product or service is the best thing for him or her all things considered, the easier it is for them to buy and the amount of effort in the close is very small. If the presentation has been poor, or if the qualification process has been poor, this may not be the right client. They may not have the right money. They may not have the right need, and so on. Well, then the closing is very difficult. An old style selling focused all the emphasis on closing, but the new style or the new model of selling is focused on building trust, identifying needs accurately, presenting your product or service specifically to satisfy the needs that have been identified, and then just asking the customer to go ahead.

Wright

What do you think has been the most significant change or addition to the sales process in recent years?

Tracy

Well, one of the things we have to realize in a market society, in which we live, the customer determines everything that we do or don't do. And the biggest change is customers have become more knowledgeable, more sophisticated, more aware, and simultaneously there have been more products and services developed to satisfy them. So sales people have to be more knowledgeable, more thoughtful, and better prepared. They have to know their product or service inside and out. They have to know the alternatives that are available to them. And especially, they have to take time to find out more about the customer before they attempt to advise the customer to buy what they are selling.

Wright

I remember back in the '80s, I used to attend all kinds of sales seminars, and I kept hearing speakers and seminar leaders, workshop leaders say the same thing, that product knowledge was only about 10% of the sales process. And I kept asking myself, "Yes, but which 10." Don't you have to know it all to use the 10 that's necessary to close?

Tracy

Absolutely.

Wright

Why do two sales people with the same education, using the same sales process, selling the same product differ in their level of success?

Tracy

Well, first of all no two people are ever the same. My experience with working with more than five hundred thousand sales people is that the most successful salespeople start a little earlier. They work a little harder. They stay a little later. They invest far more time in learning and preparation. In a recent study, they found that the highest paid sales people spend vastly more time in personal professional development listening to tapes, reading books. My conclusion is that if you are in sales and you drive around listening to the radio, basically you have no future. If you drive around listening to music, you have no future because all the highest paid sales people drive around listening to educational audio programs. That's what gives them the edge. It's almost like they are in constant mental training between calls. Poor sales people start at the last possible moment. The average sales person in America starts, really starts work about 11:00 and begins to wind down about 3:30. The average sales person makes about two calls a day. The average sales person takes long coffee breaks and lunches, leaves early. You know one of the jokes that I say is if you get onto the freeway at 3:30, you find that it is jammed. How can it be jammed? All these people don't get off work until 5:00. Well, one of the reasons it's jammed is all the sales people are on the way home to watch television because they think that after 3:30 nobody wants to talk to them, and before 11:00 people are too busy. So basically, they work far less. Take a complete idiot in selling, who is really ambitious and determined, starts early and works harder, stays later, continually learns to upgrade his skills, sees more people, and so on, they are going to run circles around the genius who starts late, quits early, and only sees a couple of people a day.

Wright

I had several sales mentors when I was younger and they all must have read the same books. Each one of them told me that in a sales situation, the first person to speak loses. Of course, I didn't believe it then and don't believe it now. But how can that be?

Tracy

Well, it's simply not true. I think there may be a misunderstanding, imagine going and sitting in front of a customer and saying nothing. Well, you'd soon be back on the streets because what you've done is you have made every effort to get through to get an appointment, to get face to face with this prospect. Finally, you meet with them and speak with them, and now, basically, you're on stage. Now, sometimes they say that when you ask the closing question, the first person to speak loses.

Wright

Right.

Tracy

And that's probably true. If you ask them, "Do you like what I've shown you so far?" Then just be quiet until you get an answer. "Would you like to go ahead with this?" Just be quiet until you get an answer. There's a saying in professional speaking called, "stepping on your lines." This means you may tell a funny story and people start to laugh and you immediately start on again. So you step on the line and you trip people up. They don't get a chance to laugh.

Wright

Right.

Tracy

So one of the best things you can do is to just ask the question and then wait patiently for an answer even if there is a lot of silence. We say the only pressure you're allowed to use as a professional sales person is the pressure of the silence after you have asked a closing or confirming question.

Wright

I definitely posed the wrong question to you, because actually it was in a closing situation once you give the presentation. However, what bothered me was that the customer loses. I've always thought the customer wins when he buys something if I have discovered his needs.

Tracy

It's poorly phrased. What it means is that if you start talking again, the customer stops thinking about buying and gets distracted.

Wright

Right.

Tracy

So that's why it's so important. Oh by the way, in life it's a very good policy when you ask a question to just wait patiently for the answer. Don't rush in and trip over the line and start talking again before the person has had a chance to respond.

Wright

I've noticed that people, when I ask them questions you know down through the years, of course I've stepped on enough lines in my life, but I've noticed that some people answer very quickly. Others take a long time before they answer. And to consider that silence anything other than thinking about it is kind of dangerous, isn't it?

Tracy

Yes.

Wright

With the entry of internet sales, how is it possible for a customer to assess his needs without a trained sales person discovering needs through examination?

Tracy

Well, I have my own internet business. I do more than a million dollars a year on the internet. It's taken several years to develop it. So I know a little bit about internet business and sales. Here's the basic rule. The internet only works to sell a product that the prospect has already determined he or she is going to buy. In other words, it is not a place where you assess a person's needs unless you are doing something as sophisticated as purchasing a computer from Dell, and even then people who buy a Dell computer using the internet are people who are very knowledgeable about exactly what they want. They are not people who are there to have their needs assessed and to be analyzed and figured out. So the only companies that are success-ful on the internet are companies that are selling specific fixed products that people have gone there to buy. Amazon is the perfect example. Nobody buys a book from Amazon because Amazon sold it to them. They go to Amazon to buy a book because it's convenient, but they already know the book their going to buy. So, the role of the internet is basically to sell a product where all of the discretion has been taken out of it. It's a specific product at a specific price with spe-cific specifications, and it has to be unconditionally guaranteed. to sell over the internet. So sales people really have little or no role in sales.

Wright

Yeah, I know. I keep forgetting one of the titles of one of your books. I have recommended it to over a thousand people. You wrote it a couple of years ago. It's the one about getting a job and making more money.

Tracy

Yes.

Wright

It's a hardback. It's only about 90 something pages, maybe a hundred pages long, but I'll tell you what, it's probably the most powerful, practical book I have ever read on the subject.

Tracy

Well, thank you.

Wright

So I tell them to go to your website and buy the book that says something about make more money and find a job.

Tracy

Actually, it is Get Paid More And Promoted Faster.

Wright

That's it! That's it! What a great book that was.

Tracy

Well, thank you.

Wright

You know I've read more books and heard more cassettes and CDs and attended more workshops and seminars on customer service than any other single topic. Yet, customer service seems to be at an all-time low. Am I over sensitive, or do we have a problem with customer service in this country?

Tracy

Well, the challenge there, you have to understand that it's very much like saying you know some people are polite and some people are rude. So it differs from person to person. And even within the same restaurant, it differs from person to person in the same business. So, it's very much a personal thing. What we have found, by the way, is that people treat their customers the way the manager treats them. So whenever you go into a place that has great customer service, you'll find that the manager is a good manager, and takes really good care of his people. It's a natural, logical expansion from the manager to the people in the company to the customers. Whenever there is poor customer service, it means you have a poor manager. The manager treats the people poorly, so they just take it out on the first people that they meet. So all over America, and in every single business, there are different levels of customer service. Some are fantastic, some are medium, some are poor, but what we know is that customers today are so demanding that if you do not treat them really well, they will go away and never come back. They will just continue gravitating like moths to a flame. They will continue gravitating toward the companies that treat them the best. That's why the companies that have the best service are the ones that are growing most rapidly.

Wright

I know that you've trained so many people in the last few years because I've watched your career just soar. I'm a real fan, and a lot of my friends have everything taped on TPN that you ever did. So I skipped a question I really wanted to ask you because I'm interested in your feelings about it. The question is, you know, perhaps sales as a vocation is more appealing than it has been in the past; however, it seems that a salesperson does not enjoy the respect and the admiration that a "professional" does. Why do you think that is?

Tracy

Well, there's two answers to that. Earl Nettier once said that there is no such thing as a good job. There are only good people doing that job. So every single job, the person who does it brings honor to the job. Let me give you a quick aside. I was at a California Pizza Kitchen not far from us. One of the people who works there as a porter and a busboy table care is a Mexican immigrant whose name is Manuel Salverago. This guy is hard working. He's got a problem with his back and his leg, so he walks with a limp. He's hard working. He's fast. He is pleasant. He is polite. He recognizes people. He's not even a waiter. He's just a busboy. He's just in motion all the time. You go there and you sit there, and I look for this, you say, "Geez, this is an incredible guy. Look at the way he does that. Look at the way he moves." And he comes up and we talk, and I always say hello to him. And he says hello, he recognizes me. And I said to the manager, "You know that's a remarkable guy there." He says, "Oh, huh, Manuel, he's the most dynamic person in this whole company." He is so respected. He's admired by everybody. He's well paid. Everybody likes him. Why? It's because he brings honor to his work. Now, let's come to sales. In sales, I've learned a very interesting paradox. In sales, it's easy to get in. Anybody can get a sales job. But that is where easy stops. Many people think because it's easy to get in, it's easy to rise. So they get a job, and maybe they have an interview a couple of times, but then they wonder why they are just not rising up like getting into an elevator and pushing a button. After you get the sales job, from then on everything is hard, harder, and harder still. Nothing is easy.

So therefore, everybody who starts off in sales, because it's easy to get in, starts off like a marathon runner way back in the pack, and then the work begins. And you have to work a long time. You know, in order to move to the top of the field, it takes five to seven years to be a master of your craft. Now this is the most remarkable thing, and it's shocking to people. Let's say if you want to be a tennis player, if you want to be a salesperson, if you want to be a lawyer, after you have learned the basic skills, it then takes five to seven years of hard work, continually upgrading your skills, continually practicing to master your craft to get into the top 10%. Now here's a couple of points. If you dedicate yourself to becoming excellent in selling, there's nothing that will stop you from eventually getting into the top 10%. In the top 10% of your field, I don't care what your business is, you're going to be one of the highest paid people in this country. You're going to be respected and esteemed by people around you. You're going to be a major force in your community. You're going to be looked up to and admired. You're going to be taking company sponsored trips. You're going to have a beautiful home and life for your family. But it's going to take you five to seven years of hard work to get there. Now here's the second point. The time's going to pass anyway. It's very important to understand the time is going to pass anyway. Five to seven years from now, five to seven years will have passed. The biggest mistake that people make, and the biggest regret they have, is why didn't I start earlier? Why didn't I start five to seven years ago and just put my head down because the time is going to pass anyway. The only difference is five to seven years from now, are you going to be at the top of your field enjoying a fabulous living, be one of the most respected people in your business, have a beautiful home and a car and a wonderful income, or are you going to be back in the pack struggling away with the 80 to 90% of the majority. But the time is going to pass anyway.

So therefore, it's easy to get into selling, but after that it's like easy to get into a huge marathon. You may have to qualify a little bit, some you don't even have to qualify. You just have to pay the entry fee. But then the race begins, and then it's a long race. That is really hard. It's not easy after that. It's only easy to get into the race, then you have to work. That's why some people make selling an honorable field, and they are the most respected people in their business. And some people just struggle away, and they've got holes in their shoes. They never read, and they never listen to audio programs. They never go to sales seminars. They come in late and they leave early, and they blame all their problems on the company or the competition, and they don't understand why they don't move ahead. But it's purely self-inflicted wounds.

Wright

I've heard a lot about personality profiles in the past few years. There are a lot of companies that have a lot on the market. Do you think one can predict with any accuracy a good person with a sales profile that will be more likely to be successful?

Tracy

Absolutely! We use sales profiles extensively, and we use them with major corporations. I did some work with a Fortune 500 Company recently. I brought in one of my experts who did a personality profile on their entire sales force. They had about eight teams working nationwide. With just the profiles, and there are three profiles, and the first profile is does this person have the personality of a salesperson? The second profile is can this person sell? Do they have the requisite skills? The third skill is will this person sell? Do they have the internal drive? And the third one is the value test. It's very important because there are people who have a great personality, but you put them into a sales situation, they collapse. So they did all three tests. They broke them and categorized them into teams. And then he explained to the senior executives, this is your top team. This is your middle team. This is your bottom team. This is what they do. This is what they say. These are their complaints. These are their successes. And they went back and forth and explained. He never even met these people. He just had them do the test, and they were absolutely astonished. He had absolutely picked out the top performers in every team, the top team in every area; their strengths, weaknesses, what they do, and he said this is your major problem within your sales force nationally. He explained that this is they're very strong on prospecting and getting the first appointment. They are very weak on closing. They are poor at their customer development. It goes on and on, and they were just shaking their heads because all of that stuff they had learned from years of experience. So yes, personality profiles are very, very important. We will never hire a person without doing a basic personality profile on them to find out if they have the personality that we require.

Wright

You know many people, and I would probably fall into this category, look for people as role models and search for successful people to become mentors as they travel the path of becoming better or a more successful salesperson. Is that thinking still useful? If so, who are some of the people that have shaped your business success?

Tracy

Well, I worked with Dr. Albert Schweitzer in Africa many years ago. Schweitzer is famous for having said, "You must teach men at the school of example for they will learn at no other." So role models are critically important for us because we need to see how it is done properly, which is true in every sport. It's true in music. It's true in everything. So what happens with human beings is we gravitate towards what we most admire. If we admire a person, then what we do is we gravitate toward emulating the behaviors of that person. If we admire men and women of courage and integrity, then what we do is we try to exemplify courage and integrity in our own lives. So role models are very important. Mentors are important as well as long as they are role models. A mentor who gives advice, who is also admired by the person receiving the advice, is going to have a major impact on that person's personality. Then the final question with regard to me is I have been positively influenced by hundreds, maybe thousands, of people over the years. You can have a mentor or role model who died two thousand years ago, or whose books you've read, or whose audio programs you've listened too. So you don't have to have direct one-on-one contact with them. Someone can write a fabulous article or a beautiful poem, and you can admire that and respect it and agree with the sentiments in that person. Then that person's views will have an effect on your personality.

Wright

When I first got into sales when I was a young fellow, I used to just take it so seriously, and you know I was probably a drag even to myself. Then I got enrolled, I mean there were records, there weren't any cassettes out yet, of a fellow named Bill Gove in Florida who used to work for 3M.

Tracy

Yeah, I know him very well. He was one of my very dear friends.

Wright

I found out that you can have a great sense of humor and still be a successful salesperson. It's not all that serious. He probably never knew that he was one of my role models, but he certainly was.

Tracy

That's great! He's a great man. He died recently, but Bill Gove was a great man.

Wright

I hated to see him passing. His passing is going to have a great impact, especially on the National Association of Speakers.

Tracy

Yes.

Wright

He was really, really admired by and respected widely by that group.

Tracy

Yes.

Wright

Finally, what word of encouragement do you have for anyone in our reading audience that might help them become more successful as they follow their career path of sales and service?

Tracy

Well, the biggest weakness we have in America is what is called the "quick fix" mentality. Everybody wants things fast and easy, and you have to get over that if you want to be successful and happy in your field. You have to realize that success takes a long time, and that you are in a race. So you are going to have to work harder than other people who want to be successful as well. You have to invest more in yourself, in learning and growing. You have to manage your time better. Above all, you have to see more people.

The great rule for success is to spend more time with better prospects, to spend more time with better prospects. The more people you see, the better you get, and the better you get, the more effective you are. The more effective you are, the more sales you make. The more sales you make the more motivated you are to see even more people. So it's what is called a positive feedback loop in psychology. If you constantly upgrade your skills and learn new things, and then try those new things with your prospects and customers, you get feedback, and you get results which motivate you to do even more of it. I'm pretty sure you'll put yourself onto an upward spiral. You must realize that everybody who is at the top today started at the bottom. Everyone who is doing well was once doing poorly. Everybody who is at the top of your field was at one time not in your field at all. What others have done, you can do as well. What others have done, you can do as well if you just learn how and just practice it until you master it.

Wright

What are you working on right now? Are you working on a book? I do want to run people to your website. It's www.briantracy.com. A lot of my friends call me and they say, "I tried to find that Brian Tracy fellow and he doesn't have a website." I say, "Well, you're misspelling it then." But anyway I would like to suggest that people go to your website for products on several different topics that I have enjoyed down through the years. But what are you working on now?

Tracy

Well, I'm just finishing up a new book. It's called *Million Dollar Habits*, and it will be out in December. I just released my latest book which is called *Change Your Thinking: Change Your Life*, and it's shipping to the bookstores as we speak. I just signed a new contract for a book called *How to Master Your Time* which will be out in march and it's going to be the best book on time management ever written. I am just getting a new contract in the mail for a book that will be out next year called *Getting Rich In America*, which is going to be a powerful book on all the different ways people go from rags to riches.

Wright

The habits book that's coming out, what is it about? Is it a how-to book?

Tracy

Oh yes, it's very practical. It shows 95% of everything that you do in life is governed by your habits, and that successful people have success habits. The habits range from the way they think about themselves to their attitudes toward their goals, setting goals each day, to their attitude toward money, toward work, toward family, relationships, health, business growth, savings and investments, and so on. It's a series of habits that people have that when you practice these habits, which you learn by repetition, you achieve more and more, faster and faster, easier and easier.

The difference in life is that some people have these success habits because they've been taught them or they've developed them, and some people have not yet learned them. The wonderful thing is that they are all learnable. So you can learn to get up a little earlier. You can learn to set priorities on your work. You can learn to write and rewrite your goals. You can learn to save and invest part of what you earn. You can learn to continually upgrade your skills. You can learn to listen better with other people. You can learn the key habits of health, and so on. What I do is I teach this. These are all the habits that are practiced by the happiest, most successful, and best paid people in our society including all self-made millionaires.

Once you develop these habits, there's a rule that everything is hard before it's easy. So developing a habit is hard, but once you develop the habit, it's easy because it's automatic. You just do it. You breathe in, you breathe out. You just follow the habit. This method becomes easy and automatic for you to do what the successful do. You'll make more progress in a week or two or in a year or two than some people make in a lifetime.

Wright

I really appreciate the time you've spent with me. Thank you so much.

About The Author

One of the world's top success motivational speakers, Brian Tracy is the author of may books and audio tape seminars, including *The Psychology of Achievement, The Luck Factor, Breaking the Success Barrier, Thinking Big* and *Success Is a Journey.*

Brian Tracy

www.BrianTracy.com

Chapter 3

BOBBI KAHLER

THE INTERVIEW

David E. Wright (Wright)

Today we are talking to Bobbi Kahler. Bobbi is a customer retention strategist, professional speaker, and author. She guides leaders and teams in sales and customer service to accelerate sales, increase customer loyalty and achieve high performance. She facilitates strategic planning sessions and is also a highly sought speaker at corporate conferences and industry associations. Bobbi is a contributing author in the best-selling book *Masters of Success* (Entrepreneur Press), and is the author of *Bring Your Business into Focus*, a small business owner's guide to growing a business. She's president of Kahler Consulting Group, the Customer Advocate Company(SM). They help companies grow through their existing best customers. Bobbi, welcome to *Conversations on Customer Service and Sales*!

Bobbi Kahler (Kahler)

Thanks! It's great to be here.

Wright

What does the Customer Advocate Company(SM) mean?

Kahler

What that means is that we help companies turn their customers into loyal advocates. We help them create strong relationships with their customers so that their customers don't even want to consider other options. In fact, I think that if we don't have a strong relationship with our customers and one that provides value to them, then our customers will continue to remain our competitors' prospects.

Wright

It seems like they're sales people that you don't have to pay.

Kahler

That's exactly right. The more customer advocates you have, the more sales and growth opportunities they can create for you.

Wright

It seems like a customer advocate is much more than just a satisfied customer then. Is that right?

Kahler

Absolutely. A customer advocate is much more. In today's market place, it isn't enough to simply satisfy customers. In fact, one recent study shows that 80% of customers who switched from one company to a competitive product or service were satisfied by their original vendor. Satisfying customers is just a minimum standard for keeping our doors open. What we need to do is to look for ways to exceed their expectations. How can we create experiences for them that makes them want to come back for more and tell others about us?

To do this, we need to think differently about service. It's about providing a service experience that gives customers the opportunity to be a part of things that are important to them, to pursue and achieve the goals they care about the most. The service that makes this possible is something a customer would want more of and would tell others about.

Sometimes, ironically, our service gets in the way of providing an ideal customer experience. Our service is there to help the customer fill a need, solve a problem or achieve a goal. We've all heard of the salesperson who loses the sale because they didn't stop talking once the customer was sold; this happens in service, too, when we haven't taken the time to identify what the customer is *really* buying. A client of mine—I'll call her Sue—just shared this story with me and it provides a great example of this. She had hired an e-business firm to help her with her website. Now, Sue doesn't know much about internet strategy nor does she want to. She wants her website to work—attract visitors, engage visitors and generate sales. The e-business company that she used kept throwing new ideas at her that she could consider, but nothing was getting done on the website and Sue didn't feel like she was receiving *answers*; instead she was receiving possibilities, not recommendations. Eventually, she had to terminate the relationship and Sue felt bad because she knows that the company put a lot of hours into the project but she just wasn't getting results. The firm seemed to believe that the more hours and the more research and the more ideas generated equaled great service; whereas, Sue, was looking for answers. It's imperative that we are thinking from the shoes of our customers. The bottom-line is that it doesn't matter if we think it's valuable; it matters if the customer thinks it's valuable.

Wright

I read on your website that you help service and sales teams identify their Blackberry. I've got to know what that means.

Kahler

Well, I don't know if you listened to the audio of the story on the website, but basically, the Blackberry concept is based on an experience that I had as a kid growing up on a farm in Missouri. I sold blackberries to my neighbors so that I could earn money for school clothes. Now what I learned from that little business was that I might have been picking blackberries, but that's not what my customers were buying. For example, one of my neighbors confided in me that they used those blackberries as a way to entice their grandkids over for a visit—that was the only way they could get their grandkids to visit. They were buying an experience, not blackberries.

So the way that I use that with sales and service teams is that I help them dig deep into the value that they are truly providing for their clients, and it's an eye-opening experience for them. What I hear afterwards from them is that they never again look at what they do in quite the same way. They have pride and confidence in their work, and they feel personally committed to their colleagues and to their customers. As a result, what I hear from their managers is that customers are much more satisfied with the interactions they have with the company—a great boost for the company reputation and brand.

Wright

How do you help your clients to dig down to the real value they provide to their customers?

Kahler

That can be quite tough for people because we're so close to it. So what I typically do is I start them thinking about their Blackberry—what their customers are really buying from them—although most people tend to start with more surface level values so it does require some digging. But it's a great way to get them to start seeing it a bit differently and focusing on what their customers get, not on what they do. And that's a critical distinction.

So, when it's necessary, I have an exercise that I use that really seems to make sense to people, and it stimulates a great discussion that leads to some powerful epiphanies. The exercise looks like this: As I mentioned, I grew up on a farm. And like most people who live on a farm, we grew tomatoes. And for some reason we always had so many tomatoes that, literally, we could have fed a small town. So we would make huge batches of tomato juice. On the day we were to make the juice, we'd go out to the garden and we'd pick several buckets of tomatoes, some green peppers, some onions and a few carrots. We'd come into the house and we'd get the biggest kettle that we had, and we would put all of the ingredients into the kettle. Then it would simmer for hours; and when it was done, we'd put the concoction through a strainer so that we could extract the juice from the pulp.

That's what we need to do here. We need to extract the juice from the pulp. The pulp represents the individual deliverables that we throw into the pot. The juice is the delicious extraction. Nobody ever wanted the pulp. They only wanted the juice. So then we discuss and record, what, for them, gets thrown into the kettle—the work they do. Their ingredients, if you will. After we finish that, we extract the value—the juice—from those ingredients. It's been highly effective. Using the e-business example from earlier, the hours spent, the research, those are just ingredients. What's the extraction? What's the juice? What's the outcome that those things achieve for the customer?

One word of caution: sometimes things will end up in the juice that should be in the kettle. For example, often someone will put in "my expertise or knowledge" into the juice. Those aren't outcomes. Those are still ingredients. So sometimes, just like when you're making real juice, you have to strain it twice.

Wright

If you were advising me to dig for my Blackberry, I would be looking for benefits that the end user would have?

Kahler

It's deeper than benefits like we normally see in marketing and sales messages. The Blackberry is the true essence of value wrapped in emotion—it's irresistible. It's that emotion that makes people buy.

Wright

Right.

Kahler

We rationalize it with reason, but it's that emotion, just like with those grandparents. I mean they were buying time to see their grandkids.

Wright

Yeah, I can remember they didn't have to bribe me to go to my grandmother's house.

Kahler

No!

Wright

In your business what has been your toughest challenge relating to sales?

Kahler

Early in my business, my biggest challenge was making the sale to myself. I think there's only one person that we ever need to convince in sales, and that's ourselves. You know, they say that you can't really love someone until you love yourself. Well, until you've sold yourself on your value, I don't think you can sell anybody else either. The consequences of not making this sale are huge: lost sales, allowing ourselves to be shopped on price, seeking out lesser opportunities because we're not confident to go after the big ones. Self-sabotage. Once you understand the value that you provide to your customers—that fundamental value that brings about positive change in their lives or in their businesses—selling, as we know it, ceases to exist. Instead of selling we are simply bringing our value to the table.

This is when we begin to make ourselves, what I call, intrinsically attractive. By that, I mean when we understand and believe in the value we provide, we have an aura of confidence—not arrogance—but that confidence exudes from us and attracts customers to us.

Think of it this way: let's say you're driving through town and you see a billboard, and it says, "Buy our bread. It's delicious." Now you might notice the billboard and you might decide to follow up. But let's say that you're driving through a neighborhood, the windows on your car are open, and you pass a bakery, and you can smell the bread baking. I mean that's irresistible. You find yourself pulling up to the bakery and buying the bread. No one tried to sell you. You decided to buy. And here's the thing: Because you decided to buy and you didn't feel like you were sold, you're more likely to be satisfied with your purchase.

From what I hear from people in the field, those who are selling and serving, making the sale to yourself is a big issue. And it's absolutely critical that we address it. The bottom-line is that both confidence and doubt are contagious. Whichever one we have, is the one that our prospects and customers will catch. If we give them doubt, they will question our value and haggle on price. If we give them confidence, they will feel good about making an investment in themselves because they will be confident that they are getting value. And, because we are confident, they will be more comfortable making the decision.

Wright

I remember when I was in junior high school there was this bakery across the street from my school. Oh my! It was horrible. I stayed hungry all the time.

Kahler

It's irresistible! You can't control it. But I think that's how we make ourselves intrinsically attractive. When I see a team—or even just a team member—struggling with this, I know that we have to address it and complete the sale. It can be challenging, but, once they "get it," once they see their value, it is so rewarding—they have the pride and confidence to become a star performer.

Wright

What are some of the challenges that you see when working with your clients?

Kahler

While every client is a bit different, I would say that one of the biggest challenges is that too often the sales person commodifies their own value. And what I mean by that is, commodify, according to my little dictionary, is when you turn something of value into a commodity. And that happens when we label ourselves into a huge group along with everybody else with nothing that explains how we make a difference for our customers. And by doing that, we're making ourselves nondescript. Think about your favorite police drama. You've probably noticed that seemingly every police car ever used in undercover work is always a nondescript blue sedan.

Wright

Right.

Kahler

And, why is it that way? So that the good guys don't get noticed. That's fine for police work, not so good for sales. So for example, in the past when someone has said, "You know, Bobbi, what do you do?" I used to say, "Well, I'm a consultant, speaker, and trainer." Not surprisingly nobody cared.

Wright

Right.

Kahler

Now I say "I'm a customer retention strategist and speaker. And what I mean by that is I help companies grow through their existing best customers." Now that gets a lot more interest, and, most importantly, it opens the conversation in the direction I want it to go. So much of this is simply being prepared. One of the tools that I share with my clients is what I call The Conversation Funnel™ which helps people think about and fine tune what they want others to know about them and their business.

Wright

That is interesting.

Kahler

Yeah! It is interesting. Something I find fascinating about it is, typically, most people enter into the exercise thinking that they know what they want to say about their business. But once we get started, it doesn't take too long before they realize that they're not prepared and they are really struggling. Then, we get some good work done. One of my clients is an insurance firm and the owner and I have been working on his Conversation Funnel™. His new comfort and confidence with conversations about business puts his prospects and customers at ease, and they are much more likely to consider his services seriously.

Wright

What are some of the perceptions or myths that you see today?

Kahler

One of the biggest, and I think potentially most frustrating for companies is that companies believe that all they have to do is just do a good job for their customers and that will turn their customers into advocates, and then the positive word of mouth and referrals will happen.

As I said earlier, doing a good job for a customer simply keeps the doors open. If we want our customers to come back and bring others with them through those doors, we need to do more, a lot more. For example, I recently did a retreat for a sales team to help them uncover new sales opportunities. They are a great company and they're growing fast. They have satisfied customers who are very happy with the service they receive; however, the company hadn't found a way to turn that satisfaction into a tangible asset—customer retention, new customer acquisition, positive PR. So we worked together to address those issues.

Obviously there's a lot that goes into that; however, here are two things that a business can look at to get started. First, what's the value they provide in the relationship with their customers and what about the on-going value? And now keep in mind this absolutely has to be from the customer's point of view. And, second, how are they continuing to invest in the relationship. I tell my clients that you want the customer to know that you care about them and their objectives. I know this sounds extremely simple and it is! Yet often it's not done.

Too often, I think, as customers we feel like it's our wallets that a company cares about. That's a big mistake. Once the customer begins to feel that way then the customer's priority becomes protecting their wallet. Actually, this happened to me as a customer just a couple of weeks ago. I had placed an order for a product, and it was inexpensive. It was under $20.00. Now the person I placed this order with was someone who I had literally spent thousands of dollars with over the last few years. The only time I hear from the person is when it's time for me to buy again. So I place my order. I got the product. No note of thanks or anything, but okay. A week later I got the same product in the mail. So I e-mailed the person right away. I didn't want their inventory to be off, and I didn't want to cheat them. At this point, there were a lot of different things this person could have done. Thank me for pointing it out and just say bring it next time I see you. Or keep it. Or I'll send you a prepaid package that you can return it. Instead, number one, I didn't receive a thank you. And I got a very short, "Well, you have to send it back to me right away." That kind of bugged me because it wasn't my mistake and now it was going to cost me time and money to correct their mistake.

To keep customers coming back, companies should genuinely care about the success of their customers and they need to demonstrate that commitment. It's not enough to proclaim it—they've got to demonstrate it. Bring the proclamation to life; otherwise, there's no reason for a customer to be loyal.

Wright

Right.

Kahler

It made me feel like dollar signs were all that they cared about. And because of that feeling, I'm not doing business with that person anymore. For a product under 20 bucks, they just lost a customer who's spent thousands of dollars. So here's a simple way to test how we're doing. How many unsolicited letters of gratitude of thanks do we receive from our clients and colleagues?

Wright

As a matter of fact, I have a ... I was trained back in the '60s to keep all the Pep Rallies that I have that people sent me, thank you notes and all like that. I have them in a big folder.

Kahler

Great.

Wright

And when I get really depressed...I go all the way back.

Kahler

Here's what I do: in my office, on one of my shelves, I have an ornamental box, where I keep all the thank you notes, letters, and printed e-mails. They make great reminders of how I'm making a difference. It's nice to look through those.

Wright

What are some of the ways that a company can distinguish themselves from their competition?

Kahler

I think that to a large extent it's through the relationships that we build with them, the relationships that we build with our customers. I know that when I'm the customer and someone has built a relationship with me, then that person, to me, doesn't have competition because there's absolutely no question as to who I'm going to spend my money with.

Companies complain about lack of loyalty on the part of the customers. What they should be doing is asking themselves, "What am I doing to deserve loyal customers?" If there's no loyalty then that is an indicator that there's no relationship. Loyalty and relationships go hand in hand.

One of the simplest things that we can do to create that type of relationship is to provide what I call an extra cup of blackberries. Obviously, this goes back to my little blackberry business. When I started that, I knew that I had one shot at converting my neighbors into customers. Where we lived it was very rural and a dollar was difficult to come by, and I knew that whenever my neighbors placed an order, I'd have to deliver more than they expected. So when they ordered blackberries, I'd always provide an extra cup of blackberries. It wasn't much, but they noticed, and they appreciated it. So you might be thinking, "Well, how important could that extra cup of blackberries be?" Well, a few years into my little business, one of my neighbors, Mae, her grandkids decided to get in on the action. They knew I was making money and they wanted a piece of it. And I thought, "Great, you know, grandkids. How do I compete with that?" I was worried, but I called Mae on the phone basically to verify that she'd be ordering her blackberries from her grandkids. And she informed me that no, she would be ordering them from me. And I was shocked. Here's what she told me: "You know, Bobbi, my grandkids went out and picked me a quart of blackberries. And you know what they did? They picked me one quart, not a single berry more, so I'll be ordering my blackberries from you." So if an extra cup of blackberries could protect me from the competition of grandkids, what can it do for us in our businesses today?

Wright

Right. I noticed on your website, and in your article in *Masters of Success,* that as a child you were told by a speech pathologist that you would never be able to speak, yet here you are a professional speaker. How does that help you help your clients?

Kahler

It helps in a few ways. First the story really helps to create change. In a big way the fact that I overcame that obstacle takes away their excuses. I remember after one presentation a sales person came up to me and he said, "You know I'm really upset with you." He was a big guy so I was kind of nervous. Then he said, "I guess that if you could learn to talk then I can get out there and make something happen." And I think that sometimes we simply need reminders that we all have our own obstacles and challenges.

Second, I use that story as a way to focus the team on the possibilities of what we can achieve. Because I think too often we get wrapped up in our present performance and that blinds us from the possibilities, from our potential. This is not to say that we ignore where we are, but rather that we believe in and we focus on where we can be.

And then finally, closely related to that is that this makes a point that each of us have a decision to make. Do we hang on to our limitations or do we reach for our potential? When I was in the eighth grade, a teacher challenged me to speak in front of the school. Now at this time I still couldn't talk. I only had six weeks to prepare. It was agonizing. I didn't want to do it, but my mom said I had to, so there you go. So I did it and I did very well at it. It was the hardest thing that I'd ever done, but I loved it. I just fell in love with it, and I know that my path to becoming a professional speaker began in accepting that challenge and deciding to reach for my potential instead of holding on to my limitations.

Wright

You know, after having booked speakers for the last 15 years of my life, I've been to seminar after seminar and workshop after workshop. I've read tons of books and had many conversations with people about the subject of customer service. And I feel, I don't know what the truth is, but I feel as if we are getting as much information on customer service as we can handle, yet customer service is at an all time low in our country and in our culture.

Kahler

That's exactly right.

Wright

Why do you think that is?

Kahler

I think that we become too focused internally and we're simply not focusing on our customers. You know, yeah, we've got databases and we keep track of all this information, but how are we using that to provide value to the customer? All the technology and automation makes us think that we're customer focused. We see a customer transaction, and so we think we can persuade them to want another one. But we're asking the wrong questions. We're asking what else the customer might buy from us instead of what we could do to help the customer be successful and feel successful. This isn't about making a sale; it is about making a customer.

Wright

Right.

Kahler

I think it's incredibly important that we get into the shoes of our customers and we think about "what would I want if I were the customer?" Go through the whole process of how the customer interacts with the company. Survey your customers. Find out what do *they* want at each of those points. What's meaningful? What's valuable to them, not to us. They're the customer. They're the driver. Too often, that's missed.

Wright

So in this book, *Conversations on Service and Sales*, we're trying to offer to the reader some real good information that can help them grow personally and corporately as well. So if you could speak to them now, the readers that is, what's one of your key pieces of advice that you would give them?

Kahler

There are two things actually. I think in addition to recognizing and believing in our own potential, we need to extend that to the people who are around us. Believe in their potential and help them achieve it. I often think about that teacher who challenged me to speak in front of the school. Clearly, she was willing to look past my present performance and she was willing to take a chance on and believe in me and in my potential. And I think that if we want to get better, if we want to serve our customers better, if we want to increase our sales, then we need to help our teams get better as well.

Second, I think that we have to understand what's really important. Too often I see people who get swept up in the search for perfection. So much so that if we aren't perfect, we get discouraged. And I think business and life are tough enough without us making it tougher.

I remember a number of years ago I was on a flight from Tulsa, Oklahoma, to Chicago, Illinois. It was both the worst and the best flight of my life. It started with my drive to the airport. It was an hour and a half drive through violent thunderstorms, and I barely made it to the airport on time. But I made it and I had to run through the airport. So I got to my seat, the flight attendants closed the door and we pushed back from the terminal. We took off and for the next 45 minutes we flew through the thunderstorms I had just driven through. It was awful. But, we finally flew out of it. Suddenly there was a very loud bang on the left side of the airplane. Three minutes after that, the pilot came on and he said, "Well, folks, you've probably noticed that we just lost our left engine." And I thought, "No, I didn't notice that. If I had, I would be freaking out and not sitting here calmly." So we had to prepare for a crash landing. Finally, we approached the airport and we touched down. It was really bumpy. It was one of roughest landings I've ever been through. But we were on the ground and we were safe. I was pretty happy. As we left the plane, the pilot was greeting people as we passed by, and as I was passing he said, "Sorry, folks, about the landing. I know it wasn't perfect." And I looked at him and I said, "I don't care if it was perfect. I care that it was successful."

Wright

Right.

Kahler

I mean I was pretty happy to be walking off that plane. And I think that it's really important that we keep our perspective. What are we striving for? Are we striving for perfection or are we striving for success? I think it's important that we keep our eye on that.

Wright

Well said. Well, this has been fun. I have learned a lot. This was a great conversation.

Kahler

I've had a good time.

Wright

Today we have been talking to Bobbi Kahler who is a customer retention strategist, a professional speaker, and as we have found out an author of *Masters of Success* and *Bring Your Business into Focus*. Bobbi, thank you so much for taking this amount of time with us today, and I've really learned a lot. I appreciate your being with us here on *Conversations on Customer Service and Sales*.

Kahler

Thanks, David. It was my pleasure.

About The Author

Bobbi is a customer retention strategist, professional speaker and author. She helps corporations grow through their existing best customers. Bobbi is known for achieving results—increased customer retention, uncovering new sales opportunities and increased profitability. She's a frequent radio guest discussing customer acquisition and retention. In addition to her books, she publishes the monthly newsletter, *The Customer Advocate Source™*, the resource for teams who want to find—and keep—more of their best customers.

Bobbi Kahler

Kahler Consulting Group

The Customer Advocate Company[SM]

4315 NE Wygant Street

Portland, Oregon 97218

Phone: 503.546.7070

E-mail: bobbi@kahlerconsulting.com

www.kahlerconsulting.com

Chapter 4

JOSEPH ROSALES

THE INTERVIEW

David E. Wright (Wright)

Today I am speaking with Joseph Rosales. Joseph is considered by many professionals in the retail service industries to be a customer service guru. For over 30 years he has been helping retail organizations improve customer service and in the process raise the bar on customer service expectations.

Joseph inspires and motivates people to improve the way they serve their customers and at the same time provides concrete solutions to the challenging tasks of achieving excellence in customer service with every customer, every day.

Joseph is the founder and president of Customer Service Solutions, Inc., an international consulting company that is dedicated to the mission of improving customer care at businesses who truly see their ability to attract, serve and retain customers as a primary key to their business success.

Wright

Joseph, thank you for taking the time from your busy schedule to speak with me today.

Joseph Rosales (Rosales)

It is my pleasure David.

Wright

Improving customer service is your main focus at your consulting business, so I am sure you could write an entire book on the subject.

Rosales

I already have...and your company published it for me.

Wright

Oh yes, I guess that will be a great lead-in to the book later, but for now tell me about your perspective on customer service in today's marketplace.

Rosales

First, let me say that my perspective on customer service has been shaped over three decades. I started my experience in customer service as a part-time sales person in a major department store. I was assigned to the men's clothing department; however, I had no experience in clothing sales. Being assigned to that department was the turning point in my young career search and set me on a path to a long and prosperous career in retail. It was in that small section of the store that I would meet two gentlemen who would influence me both professionally and personally and would become my closest friends and mentors, at that time in my life. Their influence on my earliest perspectives on sales and customer service still serve me today. Angelo Scorsone and Michael Pallan were models of effective managers and excelled at leading others to accomplish their best.

Wright

Please share a bit more.

Rosales

Certainly, they taught me the finer points of sales, merchandising and display, color coordination and good communications, but the basics are what stand out the most. For example; I learned when someone came into the store they were looking to buy something. Our job was to help them find it and make it easy for them to purchase. That generally involved helping the customer feel great and look as good as they could...and I liked making people look and feel good and at the same time, accomplishing my sales objectives. You see, they taught me that one of our most fundamental objectives as retailers is to make it easy for a customer to be a customer.

David, all of us are customers from a few to many times per week and it is not news to most of us that customer service in many companies is not what it could be. Sure there are the standouts in customer service, but those companies are the exceptions, not the rule. I am sure you would agree you have more poor to mediocre service experiences in your week than you do excellent service interactions, is that right?

Wright

Unfortunately, I have to agree.

Rosales

You see, retail has changed so much in the last 30 years. I remember back when I first came into retail there was really not much in the way of "big box" retailers like Wal-Mart, or Target and certainly there were no Sam's Clubs, or Circuit City electronics stores.

These retailers do such a good job of bulk merchandising and providing selection and low pricing on many items that they expect customers will do without a higher level of personalized service. This creates an expectation in the customer's mind that they can get a pretty good selection and the lowest prices virtually any day of the week. And they are right. But, personalized service...well that is another story.

You see, we still want personalized service. In fact, on some most basic level, we need it. As customers, we want to be appreciated and depending on the type of purchase we are making, we need someone to help us. And if someone is going to help us, then they need to care. And if they need to care...well, we get into a whole other realm of challenges.

Wright

So what is the answer? We want low prices, but we need personalized service.

Rosales

Well, now you are asking a very tough question and we certainly cannot cover such a complex and integrated issue in the short time we have here today; however, let me say this. Much depends on the type of services and products we are talking about. Most people do not need a high level of service to select their favorite toilet paper, or complete their weekly food shopping. If the isle is well organized, properly signed and the shelf has the stock on it, then the customer will most likely be taken care of. Any personal interactions may be limited to giving directions, or being friendly at the checkout counter. However, when the product, or service is elevated to a higher priced item, or the item has enough complexity that a customer may have questions about, then the game changes. And that is where the real problems occur in customer service.

Wright

Please continue.

Rosales

Most businesses that are seeking to provide good customer service rely heavily on their employees to create a positive customer experience. And while that works in some environments say for example; at Nordstrom's who is renowned for empowering their employees to exceed a customer's service expectations, it may not work at a business that for any number of reasons may not have the caliber of talent to choose from that of Nordstrom's.

For any business to provide a higher level of customer service excellence there are three key components that must exist; First, the right people with the right service attitude. Second, a properly imaged and merchandised facility that supports a comfortable experience. And third, effective systems and processes that support an excellent service experience.

To illustrate the simplicity of these components let me ask you a few questions.

Have you ever been to a business where the person serving you filled your need, but acted in a manner that inferred they didn't really care about you as a customer, or even worse were rude, or indifferent toward you?

Wright

Yes.

Rosales

Have you ever been a customer at a business where the sales associate was very nice, but could not fill the need for an item you would expect them to have in stock?

Wright

Unfortunately, too many times.

Rosales

How about an experience in a restaurant when the server was nice and the food was good, but the restaurant was so dirty, or smoke filled that you just could not feel comfortable being a customer there?

Wright

Been there too.

Rosales

Well David, in the first instance the sales associate had what you needed, but failed to treat you with the most basic customer service element…respect. This is a failure of the sales associate.

In the second situation, the sales associate was nice enough, but for some reason could not satisfy your needs. Exceptional customer service cannot happen if you don't ultimately meet the customer's need. A friendly sales associate failed to provide for the customer, but they were very nice, while failing. In this instance, it may be a system, or failure to follow a system that failed to have the item in stock for the customer.

And in the third situation the server was nice and the food was good, but the environment in which the customer was being served was not clean, or comfortable. This is obviously a facility imaging failure.

So, each of these customer service failures is the result of a person, a system, or a facility that failed to support the customer service objective.

Wright

I guess what you are saying is that great customer service is more than just being nice.

Rosales

Precisely David.

Wright

So in your opinion, how does a business go about achieving this "holy grail" of excellent customer service?

Rosales

Well, certainly for any business to attain excellence in service they must first have a vision for it. Every great business, product, enterprise, or endeavor has started with a vision. A company must start with a vision for excellent service if they want to achieve that level of service. I truly believe if you can think it, if you can envision it, you can achieve it.

The vision for excellent service must include the type of people that would serve customers with excellence. From their personal character traits, to grooming, attitude and experience. Just imagine perfect employees serving your customers and then write down what you see. Then start recruiting and hiring and training toward this vision. The employees are what makes customer service magic happen. Your employees are quite possibly the most important component in the customer service equation .

The next part of your vision must include a very clear picture of the facility in which the customer will be served. Imagine the colors, lighting, signage and overall design. Don't be concerned about what you have now...have a vision for excellence...exceed your own expectations!

And the final part of the matrix for excellent customer service is the systems and processes that support excellent customer service. For some people this is one of the most challenging aspects of attaining a higher level of customer service excellence. Part of the process is identifying the best practices in your business and then documenting them into your service processes. For everything you do, there is a best way and a worst way to do it. As professional retailers, we must seek out those best ways and avoid the worst ways. It is a simple, yet integrated process.

Wright

I have read your book titled *Customer Service is a Contact Sport*. It is a very interesting title. Tell me, why that title?

Rosales

My book was inspired by the importance of contact. Contact is so much a part of the communications process that occurs during customer service interactions. Whether the contact is face-to-face, or on the telephone, or even over the internet, contact happens and creates impressions in the customer's mind. And impressions create buying decisions.

Wright

This is very interesting, please continue.

Rosales

From eye contact, a smile, or a handshake to the words spoken, body language, or laughter. Every contact we make with a customer sends a message...I care, I like you, I appreciate you...or I don't.

You see David, every contact makes an impression. The only choice we have is; will the contact and subsequent impression be positive, or negative? Even being quiet is an impression, isn't it?

Wright

Yes, quiet can make a very loud impression. How do you think customer service affects sales?

Rosales

Well David, people buy from people, and they generally buy more often from people they like, trust and respect. These feelings of liking, trusting and respecting that customers develop are arrived at by many different impacts and impressions.

Certainly one must be able to meet the needs of the customer; however, once those basic needs are met, the rest is all about do I like doing business with you?

As I said earlier, meeting and exceeding a customer's needs requires one to be more than just nice. We must accommodate many of the customers most basic relational needs in addition to providing for the product, or service they need.

Wright

So, how do you develop those skills in people that get customers to like, trust and respect them?

Rosales

There are many great sales training organizations out there that teach the structures of relationship building and I believe that most people can learn to improve their relationship building skills. It is really a skill, not an art. However, I believe it all boils down to a couple of basics. The ability to listen to a customer and understand what they need and want followed by the ability to communicate with and support a customer.

Yes, there are strategies that teach people how to qualify, determine wants and needs and demonstrate features and benefits. And these strategies work. Nonetheless, it is people who make strategies work and the whole process takes on another level of effectiveness when someone who has a love for serving others employs it. After all, isn't the ultimate goal of sales training to gain confidence and trust with a customer and ultimately provide for their needs?

Wright

Yes, it is.

Rosales

You know David, one of greatest problems we see in every area of sales training and in any training program for that matter, is the issue of applying the solutions that will lead to improvement long enough for them to have a positive impact on the performance that is being targeted for improvement.

For example, say someone has decided they want to improve their physical appearance and health. They may start a new exercise program. Maybe they go out and buy an instructional program on CD and they even buy some workout gear and new shoes. The initial excitement and energy that is generated is a very positive thing and is essential to achieving the results. In spite of this, what all too often happens is a short-lived effort at improvement. The individual works at the program for a week, or two and maybe other things start to interrupt the convenience of the exercise program. Maybe work schedules, family activities, social commitments, or maybe just plain old L.I.F.E. We have all been there... we have good intentions, but sticking with the program means sacrifice and commitment.

Wright

I certainly can relate to that.

Rosales

And, this becomes even more difficult if the results we are looking for have not yet been achieved. And results often don't come from most improvement programs within the first couple of weeks. So, even though the program was right and the initial commitment was made, if one doesn't stay on the path to the improvement long enough, then they will most likely stop short of the desired result. So, what then occurs is a negative result. The investment was made, the initial commitment was made, the effort was made, but the desired results were not attained.

This is a situation we too often see in business. One desires to improve a skill. They hear of a seminar that speaks to their improvement issue. They pay the fee and make the commitment to attend and while at the seminar they gather some good information. They are inspired and leave the session committed to make some positive changes. They get back to their daily routine and maybe they even try a couple of the things they have heard. Maybe some of it works. But, as with the exercise program, quite often LIFE settles in and the commitment for improvement is replaced by many other things that vie for their attention... and soon they are not on the improvement path.

You see David, *improvement is not an event, it is a process*. There is not a seminar, book, or tape that can improve one's performance unless an improvement processes is applied long enough for the improvement to occur. Improvement is really that simple, or that complicated, depending on the choices one makes.

Wright

What a great conversation. Today we have been talking to Joseph Rosales. Joseph is the founder and president of Customer Service Solutions, Inc., and as we have found out today, knows a great deal when it comes to customer service. Joseph, thank you for taking the time to talk with us today on this very important, yet widely ignored subject of customer service.

Rosales

Your welcome, David. Thank you.

About The Author

Joseph Rosales, founder and president of *Customer Service Solutions, Inc.,* helps businesses succeed by improving customer service and sales through specialized attention to people, facilities and processes.

With more than thirty years experience in retail business development and training, Joseph is a highly requested speaker, monthly columnist for various publications and author of the best-selling book *Customer Service is a Contact Sport*™.

Joseph Rosales

Customer Service Solutions, Inc.,

Phone: 800.268.9899

Email: jrosales@customerservicesolutions.com

www.customerservicesolutions.com

Chapter 5

READ BRADFORD

THE INTERVIEW

David E. Wright (Wright)

Today we are talking to Read Bradford. In 1957 while a junior at Indiana University, Read was flown to Washington, D.C., to present his humorous entertainment and to emcee a pre-inaugural ball at the second inauguration of President Dwight Eisenhower. Since that time Read had been building careers in speaking and in sales. Read served as chairman of the Speakers Advisory Bureau for the Illinois Office of Public Instruction. He was hired by the U.S. Department of Commerce to speak to regional meetings of the Office of Business Services and was then hired by the Office of Business Services to speak to industry. Read travels the country speaking to conventions, banquets, dinners, and sales meetings. He speaks most often before mixed audiences and presents a fast moving very entertaining program with the right touch of message. Read Bradford, MBA, is CEO of Bradford Systems Corporation of Chicago, a leading company in records and information management. He and his wife, Judie, reside in Golf, Illinois. Read, welcome to *Conversations on Customer Service and Sales!*

Read Bradford (Bradford)

Thank you, David.

Wright

You know it seems that every time I watch television and a salesman is portrayed, the image is always negative. For example, crooked
as a used car salesman. Yet I have heard statistics as high as 87% of
all money that passes hands in the United States is directly or indirectly traceable to some sales event. How do you view the sales
profession?

Bradford

I had not heard that statistic that you just quoted, but I have no
reason to doubt it. I think the quality of our sales profession, for one
thing, is one of the great differences between the U.S.A and most
other developed countries. I think we have more great sales people
and I think that's one of the big reasons that we have by far the
strongest economy. I think of sales people, as people with a strong
work ethic. I think in general, they are smarter than the average,
smarter than most. I would also quickly add that to be successful in
sales, a person needs to be self-directed and self disciplined. And
that's probably what separates most sales people from the people who
would like to be in the sales profession, but tried it and didn't make
it, or will not even try it. We also know that we need to be able to
overcome rejection. And I think it is rejection when we lose a sale. A
lot of the sales trainers and sales motivators will say that we should
not take a lost sale personally. I take it personally. If they don't buy
what I recommend to them, then in effect they've said, "No, Read, we
don't believe you. We believe someone else," and I do take it personally. And another thing is that I think most successful sales people
love to win and hate to lose. I also, if I can go a little further here, I
believe that in business to business selling, the sales profession positions you as being an out-sourced staff person for the buyer. If he's
looking at three different proposals that he is considering, he's going
to buy from one and not buy from two. And he wants to make the one
he buys from the person that he can most depend upon to handle this
project and make sure that the things that he wants to accomplish
get will done. I also would add in the same vein that sales people become an immense source of information. Let me relate what I think
are some dramatic examples. Sales people tell architects which products to specify and why. Sales people go into the surgical suite and

advise the doctor while he's performing surgery. I had dinner with a young lady who works for Siemens, and she had placed a note on her door that she might be up to an hour late for our dinner appointment, and she was. She jokingly says when you ask what is her business, she will answer that she sells nails and screws. But the nails and screws she sells are put into peoples' bones to hold them together during the healing process, and she stands right beside the surgeon and directs his every activity with her products. That's why she was late. Another little example is in our business, we provide records management expertise for companies that don't have records managers. So a big part of what I think of when I hear a reference to the sales profession is that it is people who gather information and then encourage action and are willing to take responsibility for their recommendations. Among other things, this requires above average intelligence.

Wright

Well, I've also prided myself on being a professional salesman, and now you tell me I am above average in intelligence. Is that across the board?

Bradford

I certainly believe that successful sales people would test out well above average.

Wright

If I were to choose sales as my profession, what would be my first consideration to begin sales activities?

Bradford

I think everyone should give a lot of thought to what they as an individual can add to any position they are considering. Some of the first questions that I would ask myself are: Am I going to be selling a commodity? Can I make a difference? Can I add value to this product? Am I going to be selling a product or service, and have six competitors who are selling essentially the same thing? What am I going to be able to do to differentiate myself from potential competitors? Am I going to be able to deliver faster than others can or will I be able to provide services that others cannot match? What can I accomplish in this profession, at this company, with these products? What talents or expertise can I bring to the customer? Let me make a little takeoff on the old slogan during one of the past presidential campaigns, "It's the economy, stupid." In one sense from the sales person's view, "It's the marketing, stupid." Marketing positions the sales person. The key question is: "If I'm going into sales, who does the marketing? Do I do it? Does the company I'm joining perform the marketing functions? Are there vendors for that company that are running ads for their products and creating leads?

Let me give you an example. A very good friend of mine, Russ Williams, sells here in Chicago for the Tom James Company. The Tom James representative comes into your office and takes your measurements. He will sell you any clothing needs you might have. He or she will help you select everything from suits and shirts to shoes and ties, and so on. I've used this example talking to a number of sales people. The Tom James Company has a structure for a salesperson that is very well defined. They provide their own marketing activity, which requires extra talents. After 3:00 or 3:30 pm in the afternoon, you make 77 dials on the telephone. You'll probably reach around 17 people. You should get seven appointments for the next day, five existing customers and two new customers. If you do that every day, you'll make $80,000.00 or $90.000.00 a year or more with the Tom James Company, and that's their daily process.

I think a salesperson looking at a sales position needs to know what is taking place here. What do I have to do? I would even ask, before I take a new sales position, "Who are your newest sales people, and do you mind if I have a talk with them?" I would do that for the same reason that prospects want to call our customer to find out if what we say is really true. Next question I'd ask is how do you differentiate yourself? How does this company differentiate itself? How do the other sales people differentiate themselves? How do they stand out? Let me give you an example. Most sales people spend their lives justifying a higher price for their product than their competitors' price. I don't believe, David, I have ever heard a sales trainer or motivator who did not devote a major part of his presentation telling how to overcome the price objection. When I was a young man selling school furniture, the big company in that product was the American Seating Company. They are still in business in Grand Rapids, Michigan. They were a huge company in the school furniture business and had the production capacity to equip the nation's schools. However, there were a couple of brothers down in Conway, Arkansas, whose family name was Virtue. They started a company called Virco. They had a totally different sales approach. The Virco sales persons' job across the country was simply to come in, see the school business manager, show the product, and get on the approved bid list. Then the Virtue Brothers would be the low bidder. They put American Seating out of the school furniture business. I don't think American Seating Company still makes school furniture. They're still in business. They're making office furniture, but they'd better run fast because the Virtue Brothers, Virco, is making office furniture also. The point I'm trying to make is that in the sales profession, there are a lot of different worlds and you need to know what is going to be expected of you. How can you make a difference in this industry? And in the case of Virco, your sales job was to become accepted as an equal for the bidding process, not to demonstrate that your product is worth more than someone else's.

Wright

You know every job I've ever taken has had its downside. Could you tell our readers what obstacles they would encounter in sales?

Bradford

The big one is time, your time and the customer's time. Making the best use of your time is a huge challenge. Vince Lombardi used to say that the Green Bay Packers never lost a game. Unfortunately, on some occasions when the whistle blew and the clock ran out they had a lower score on the scoreboard than their opponent did. But, that was because they had failed to execute their game plan as it related to the game time. If you would let them play another five minutes or so, they'd be back ahead in the score. Then let the game end. The problem, of course, is that neither Vince Lombardi nor the salesperson can determine when time is called. Many customers don't have time to see us. They used to. They don't now. Why? Because five million middle management jobs have been eliminated across the United States, and we're often, as a salesperson dealing with a department head who has the need, but doesn't have the authority to make the purchase. So the decision may go to someone higher up that we often don't get to see. We are risking our time without knowing the authority level of the person with whom we are dealing. He may not have the time to fully inform himself on all of the available options. Therefore, sales people are in the business of saving the customers' time and saving our time, because in the final analysis that's how we get paid – for our time.

Then, of course, there's the competition, but it's not just our direct competition, it's also indirect competition. Everyone who wants to sell anything to that same customer is trying to get a share of his time. So our challenge, our obstacle to overcome, is to make the customer's choice in our product category an important one. He may care about the details of his phone system, but doesn't care about his source for office furniture. He'll take bids on that. He doesn't care. But the phone system is technical. It's a product that he's going to depend more perhaps on the salesperson and his technical support people. However, in office furniture, the product often is not just independent desks and chairs, but a panel system forming cubicles. Now we're into something that is more complicated, and the sales person becomes much, much more important. Some customers aren't willing to open themselves up to suggestions, let alone to advice. Depending upon the complexity or technical aspects of the product, he may need a lot of help, but he may not be willing to take it because he feels that he would be opening himself up too much, and would become too dependent on the salesman. That's an obstacle to the sales person who wants to be an important source of information to the customer. We must become able to make the customer comfortable getting important information from us. This is what is going to position the sales person as a professional.

Wright

You know that customer service is not all about disgruntled customers, but could you tell us a little bit about the best way or ways to handle an irate customer?

Bradford

Well, David, what I'm going to say here is not going to sound particularly new and original, but I'll answer that maybe a little deeper in the same vein that most other people would state. If you have an irate customer on the phone or one who is talking to you in person, the first thing you do is totally say nothing and become the best listener you can be. Focus your eyes on his or her eyes and listen thoroughly to everything they say. Let them get it all out, every last detail. Then, from that point forward, overwhelm them with a genuine response that is totally sincere and sympathetic to their situation. Read that person a little bit. He may be the kind of person that wants you to simply step in and solve the problem. He may want you first to empathize a little bit, or a lot, and then acknowledge the pain that they have suffered. Then solve the problem. Consider this as an approach: maybe you should become more upset than he is. You are really offended by what your company has done and maybe what you have done. You are embarrassed. You are fit to be tied. You're ready to go back to the office and tear the place apart.

You may become more upset yourself than he had been, and he might start feeling sorry for the company, and try to calm you down a little bit. I remember a time at Central DuPage Hospital, where we had installed electric high-density equipment to store medical records. When the records people walked across their carpet and pushed the button to move the carriages, they got a shock. Well, that was extremely embarrassing to the medical records manager, and she had taken all kinds of criticism and complaints from her records people. And she said, "Convert this thing from electric to a manual system." And she issued our sales person a purchase order for over $9,000.00 to convert it down from electric to a mechanical assist system. I went there to see her. I believed that we could solve the problem if we put a strip of anti-static carpet of a particular kind in front of the system. Then all the static electricity would dissipate before the records people touched the electric controls. I knew that she didn't want to hear any ideas that I might have to solve the problem with the existing electrical system. So I kept quiet and let her tell me about all that she had been through. When she was finished I waited for her to calm down and then I waited for the right moment. I looked her right in the eye and said, "I'm not here to help me, I am here to help you! I've got a $9,000.00 purchase order. I'm ready to tear it up. I'm here to help you, and electric operation is better for you. Let me try this carpet idea we have and if you aren't totally satisfied, I'll be happy to convert the system." And so she let us try the carpet, and it worked fine, and she was far better off with electric operation. So waiting for the right moment and meeting the issue thinking of the customer, instead of thinking of myself worked. I had improved the whole situation. And I even came out as her hero. Where did I win by tearing up a $9,000.00 purchase order? We sell up to electrics. We don't want anyone to convert from electric to manual or mechanical assist for any reason.

Wright

Does product knowledge go hand in hand with sales skills? I mean, can you compare selling ability with product knowledge?

Bradford

That's a good question. I think in different situations one is important and in other situations the other. Let me think about that a second. No customer, no office person, no company executive comes to work in the morning and says to himself, "Boy, I sure hope a real slick salesman calls on me today. I mean I hope someone who really can manipulate a conversation and control it, will walk into my office and get me to buy something that I really didn't need to buy." No one thinks that. No one is looking for a great salesman to come in the door. But he may walk in that morning and many other mornings and have frequents thought like, "I hope someone can come in and help me solve this or that problem." "I hope someone can come in and straighten out our blankety-blank phone system." "I hope someone can come in and show me whether I should buy trucks or lease trucks." "I hope someone will come in and straighten out this office mess that we have."

So the customer is looking for knowledge and expertise, and is not looking for sales ability. But sales ability is king when the customer doesn't realize there are better ways, and he needs a creative person to come in and find better ways to do what needs to be done. For instance, 75% of office files are stored in filing cabinets, but shelf filing is a far better system. It is far less expensive, saves a lot of space and is far more efficient. But the salesperson, some salesperson, has to explain that or the customer will just keep buying filing cabinets along with his office furniture. Product knowledge is king. The more technical the product, the more important product knowledge becomes. Selling ability includes timing as does marketing. You must be there or be represented strongly when the decision is made. The good sales person understands timing. Product knowledge can create the motivation for your champion in that company. The guy that's fighting for you to see that you are awarded the contract.

Wright

Are there characteristics that a salesperson must have? In other words, what abilities should sales people try to develop and master?

Bradford

Well, I think every expert in the field will rank empathy at the top of the list of characteristics for a salesperson. You've got to have the ability to empathize with the customer, to put yourself in his or her place. Certainly, listening ability. Let me give you an example. I was watching Tim Russert on *Meet the Press*. And I don't want to get us lost in the political atmosphere that is always going on, but I heard John Kerry say that he voted against Richard Nixon's war in Viet Nam. Well, I'm old enough to remember that we went into Viet Nam under John Kennedy. And we all know that the Viet Nam War was greatly expanded by Lyndon Johnson. And we know that we exited Viet Nam under Richard Nixon. And I'm sitting there waiting for Tim Russert to jump down John Kerry's throat. But what was Tim doing, David? He was preparing his next question.

Wright
Right

Bradford
He wasn't listening. And we do that as salespeople far too often. The customer is saying something, and we're thinking about what we're going to say next.

Wright
Right.

Bradford
Instead we should totally zero in on what he is saying. Okay, another characteristic is, and this I think comes out of empathy, don't allow the customer to make a purchasing mistake, even if it means he places the order with someone else. Don't allow him to make a mistake. Look at the medical profession. First do no harm. He could lose his job over a major mistake. If you don't have the right product, say so. Don't let him make a purchasing mistake. The next characteristic I think of and maybe this is even bigger than being empathetic is work ethic. Finish every day. If you play golf, the coaches will say finish, finish the shot, finish the stroke, finish with your club head up. Finish. Every golf shot is an acceleration of the club as it meets the ball. The club head is accelerating in every golf shot whether it's a drive, a putt, a chip, or a fairway shot. There is no exception to that, and selling is very similar to that. Good selling requires a constant of acceleration on behalf of the customer. You are always accelerating his needs, what you are doing for him. And your work ethic tells you that when you get home that evening, before you turn in, before you start out the next morning, you finish everything you need to do based on what happened today so you start the next day free of all of

that. Whether you're sending e-mails out, whether you're sending notes out to somebody, whether you're leaving phone messages that someone will hear the next day, or whether you're writing up an order and mailing it, finish every thing every day.

Wright

When you're helping a customer, what are the most important qualifying questions that must be asked?

Bradford

Well, I'm going to have to draw on some of the great questions that I have learned from other people in addition to some perhaps that I've thought of myself. One of the best questions that I ever heard anyone give salespeople to use is when you are talking to a customer about a product or a service that you are selling, ask him if he does not purchase this, what is his alternative? What will he do if he doesn't go through with this purchase? If the answer to that question is, "Well, we'll pretty much keep doing what we've always done," you're probably not going to make a sale. The answer to that question needs to be, "Well, we're in deep trouble. We're running out of space. We're running out of time. We're running out of this or that, and we will not be able to complete our assignment. We need to do something different. We need to add this. We need to have this. We need to take advantage of this product or service." Another question is, "Can he buy this product from me?" If you're my customer, Dave, in so many words, I'm going to ask if you are able to buy this product from Read Bradford at Bradford Systems? Now I couldn't in my mind imagine anybody who would not be able to say "Yes" to that. Of course, they could buy from us. But we had a very good man in our company, Dennis Cropsey. He spent the greater part of six months working with three or four different departments at a major defense contractor located in Rockford, Illinois. Dennis proposed four categories of products to them. In at least three of them his product, our product, was far superior and very competitive. In the fourth case, we were right in there. He got zero in business. He got nothing. And it turned out that every purchase they made, they bought from a Rockford company, and it turned out that was their company policy. They didn't tell us that, and we didn't ask. Why would we assume that there was anyone who could not buy from us? But, someone higher up in the company caused them to make purchases that were obviously inferior.

Okay, another good question, do you have a budget? Does what we've talked about in general fit your budget? Are you comfortable with these numbers? Because it may be, first of all that they do not have it in the budget, and he's talking about something for next year or the year after. So that's a very important question. I like this one. What do we want to accomplish when we do this? And you notice I used the word "we" twice. It's not what do "you" want to accomplish or what would "you" like to accomplish? What do "we" need to accomplish? What do "we" want to accomplish with this? And I want to hear all of the things that he thinks are important. And then, of course, what's your time frame? I asked that today. I'm working on a major project now. What's the time frame? He said, "Two months." I said, "Wow! We've got to move fast." I could have been working at a normal pace or just talking with him, and now we need to move into an emergency mode. For him to do what he wants to do in sixty days, he and I have got to do a lot of fast work. Now let me give you one last question that I think of right now. This is my twist on an old question. The old question is: Who else do I need to see to make this sale? I don't like that, David. I don't like that at all.

Wright

Right.

Bradford

That infers that you're going to see his boss or somebody more important than he is, and it also infers that you're the one that needs to do it. He can't. So I say, "Who else do we need to bring along with us on this project?" I think that is a lot better way of phrasing it. Now he and I as partners are looking for an ally, and deciding which other person(s) do we need to sign off on this thing. I never make it sound like I'm going to go over his head, or that I'm needed to do something he can't do.

Wright

You know I've heard several sales trainers say that the customer is always right. Is that really true?

Bradford

David, you just hit on one of my favorite subjects. I know, and anybody who's been in business to business sales, knows that the customer is often wrong, and sometimes he's wrong at the top of his voice. The idea that the customer is always right, I think, started with Marshall Field. I can picture Marshall Field standing in his store, exhorting his sales clerk to, "Give the lady what she wants." If she wants Shalimar perfume, don't talk about Channel No. 5. The customer is right. She knows what she wants. Give the lady what she wants. Sell her Shalimar. Okay, but I'm talking now about business to business sales. And warehouses across the country are full of purchasing mistakes. A great many times the customer makes the wrong purchase. Often he may think he knows more than the salesperson who is calling on him. He generally does not because, of course, the salesperson is making his living by being an expert in the field. But again, he's protecting himself from opening himself up too much. Okay, why is the customer often wrong? Well, first of all, I would say the main reason is that he bought on low bid. I would guess that more purchasing mistakes are made in the name of buying on low bid than any other single reason. Surprisingly, another reason the customer often is wrong and makes a mistake is that he didn't buy on low bid. He paid a premium for a product that was not a premium. So the purchasing decision is often in the hands of someone who is totally unable to evaluate the products, especially if the product is complicated or technical. He needs to depend on a salesperson, and that salesperson needs to position himself as an expert who will give help and not take advantage of him and will save the customer from being wrong.

Wright

You know many of our readers will be in sales or thinking about it. Can you suggest a few good habits that would help a salesperson's career?

Bradford

Well, I mentioned work ethic a little earlier, and I'll say that again. I've mentioned empathy. We need to form the habit of being empathetic about our business and about the people with whom we work. Creative thinking outside the box should be easier for sales people because we are outside the box. The customer is inside his company box. We're outside. Also we've had the exposure of many, many, many other people that we have dealt with, companies similar, companies different from this particular customer, and we should be able to bring outside of the box creative thinking. And that's a good habit. I said to the guy I was with this morning, "I want to consider all aspects, all options." I consider even some that he thought we would discard right off. We're looking at what are we going to get for X number of dollars, and I need him to know that I'm looking out for that, just as he is.

I think we also need to make the sales process fun, fun for us and fun for the customer. We need to form the habit of studying how we make our living. Now let me give you something a lot of people may be a little uncomfortable hearing. I'm not interested in forming a habit of knowing how well the individuals on the Chicago Cubs make their living. I have a friend in the sales business and if you ask him the name of the second baseman of the Cubs, he won't have to think a second. That's nothing; ask him his batting average, that's nothing. He knows that off the top of his head. Ask him details of his products, and he will stumble. We need to make a habit of becoming more of an expert by reading and observing events in our industry. Learning things that we can bring to people. Let me quote Earl Nightingale. I used to enjoy Earl's recordings. Earl says that the average person spends four and a half hours a night watching television. According to Earl Nightingale, the late Earl Nightingale, if you cut that to three and a half hours, I think he said a panther lean and hungry three and a half hours, you could spend the other hour on your business. You could spend that one hour, becoming more knowledgeable, getting things done or building your expertise. One hour a night, seven nights a week, and in a very short time will you become one of the industry's leading experts. And you'll be the only person in your company doing that even if you work for IBM or General Motors. Good habits go back to the word 'finishing'. Finish each day's assignments that day. If you have kids in school, do family homework together. What an image that is! Another quickie for habits, I am always on time. I'm always on time. If a customer has to wait for me to come to his office, he may think he'll have to wait for my product or services. Something else that may be a little bit unique to me, as a habit, I avoid specials that could cause problems.

Wright

You avoid what?

Bradford

I avoid specials. I avoid getting trapped into furnishing something that is not what we normally do. Now, I'll put an asterisk on that. I do like to combine standard products from non-related companies to be able to furnish a bundled product that looks to my customer and to my competitors as though it's a special. But it was really standard products from unrelated companies. Other than that, if it's a real special, you've got to qualify just how important this customer is and you must realize that a special will require a lot of your time to oversee. Do not get sucked into working on a special just because we all want to jump on anything the customer throws in our direction. You must overly qualify the time it's going to take, the cost it's going to take, and the potential problems that's could come of it.

Wright

Your knowledge of sales and customer service is obvious. Can you discuss the differences as well as similarities between customer service and selling?

Bradford

Yes, let me think of that for a second. Customer service means being in the business of getting your customers to come back to you. Customer service is continuous, and it is interwoven in the sales business. In sales, we're proposing what we're going to do. In customer service, we're performing. In customer service, you're proving or hopefully not, you're disproving that you can and will do what you say. I was taught that a satisfied customer will tell no one about you because that's what he expected; that if he is extra pleased, he'll tell seven or eight people. And if he is dissatisfied with what you did, he'll tell between 25 and 30 people. So customer service cannot be separated from sales because it follows the salesperson. I was installing a project last week. It was a small project, $4,000.00. It was in the room where I have a $180,000.00 installation of the same product. I didn't personally install any of the big project. I didn't need too. But, this little one was tricky, and it had too be installed just so. Some decisions would have to be made during the installation. And so without really thinking it was a big deal, I went there personally, removed my tie and my jacket, rolled up my sleeves, and our top installer and I put in this little installation. It took us about four hours. The boss, the person who had purchased from me, had an appointment and left and wasn't there when I finished. Her assistant said to me that when her boss left, she mentioned how impressed she was that I was there personally.

And to me that was customer service, it just comes natural. There were some things about that installation that I couldn't be sure would happen unless I was there. Now let me say one last thing on this subject. My company has been in business 36 years. We're in our 37th year now. We've sold a lot of product and most of the products we have sold the warranty expired after a year. The factories that manufactured these products no longer warranty them or guarantee them in any way. We do. Every one. If you bought from me 36 years ago, even if you abused the product, if it is not properly performing to your satisfaction today, our customer service people will take care of it. That is the best advertising a company can have. I lost an order 23 or 4 years ago, to a low bid. Our price was $200,000.00, the competitor's price was $198,000.00, and it was technical equipment. And the company that sold it really couldn't support it very well. The customer had a lot of problems. I heard about the problems, and so I wanted to go and see it for myself. And I did. And when I was talking to the user, she went on and on and on about all of the negative things about the company they had bought from and the product that they had furnished. So I said to her, "Isn't there anything they do right?" And she said, "Yes, their service manager, Rich Kahle, keeps this equipment operating somehow." I said, "That's interesting. I hired Rich Kahle, and he's been our service manager for probably 23 or 24 years, and we give the best service, the best customer service in our industry. Our sales people know that. It creeps into their conversation. Every time our installers finish an installation, Rich comes around personally and inspects it and writes up a report. We don't have a competitor doing that, David. We don't have one competitor that does that. But we do it on every installation, and therefore, there is no customer of ours who has not met our customer service person.

Wright

Well, what an interesting conversation. Every time I talk to you I learn more, Read.

Bradford

Well, that's nice of you to say.

Wright

It's such a pleasure. Today we have been talking to Read Bradford. Read is an MBA, he is CEO of Bradford Systems Corporation of Chicago, a leading company in records and information management. He travels the country speaking to conventions banquets, dinners, and sales meetings; and he speaks most often before mixed audiences and presents a fast moving very entertaining program with the right touch of message. And as we have found out today, he has some message for us. Thank you so much, Read, for being with us today on *Conversations on Customer Service and Sales.*

Bradford

Thank you, David.

About The Author

Today we are talking to Read Bradford. In 1957, while a junior at Indiana University, Read was flown to Washington, D.C., to present his humorous entertainment and to emcee a pre-inaugural ball at the second inauguration of President Dwight Eisenhower. Since that time Read had been building careers in speaking and in sales. Read served as chairman of the Speakers Advisory Bureau for the Illinois Office of Public Instruction. He was hired by the U.S. Department of Commerce to speak to regional meetings of the Office of Business Services and was then hired by the Office of Business Services to speak to industry. Read travels the country speaking to conventions, banquets, dinners, and sales meetings. He speaks most often before mixed audiences and presents a fast moving very entertaining program with the right touch of message. Read Bradford, MBA, is CEO of Bradford Systems Corporation of Chicago, a leading company in records and information management. He and his wife, Judy, reside in Golf, Illinois.

Read Bradford

Bradford Systems

8700 Waukegan Rd., Suite 212

Morton Grove, Illinois 60053-2104

Phone: 847.965.5070

FAX: 847.965.5247

Email: ReadB@Bradfordsystems.com

www.bradfordsystems.com

Chapter 6

DON HUTSON

THE INTERVIEW

David E. Wright (Wright)

Today we are talking to Don Hutson. For more than 30 years, Don has been in the business of making people believe they can do better and giving them the skills to do it. He energizes audiences into action and is known for delivering real solutions for business professionals. While he has earned the reputation as a motivator, Don provides more than a cheerleading session. He empowers audience members with the skills and cutting edge strategies needed to succeed in today's business environment. Humor and great stories to reinforce ideas are Don's stock in trade. Don is CEO of U. S. Learning based in Memphis, TN. Don Hutson is the recipient of the following awards and honors: He is past president National Speakers Association, CSP Certified Speaking Professional, CPAE Speakers Hall of Fame Award, 1999 Consummate Speaker of the Year Award, SMEIs International Speakers Hall of Fame, St. Jude Hospital's Humanitarian Award, and member of the Speakers Round Table – twenty of the greatest and most successful speakers in the world today. Don is the only speaker today who has earned or been awarded all of these distinctions. Don Hutson, welcome to *Conversations on Customer Service and Sales*!

Don Hutson, (Hutson)

Thank you, David. I'm pleased to be involved in this project.

Wright

Let's begin with customer service. Many people say that they've never seen so much training on customer service in the past few years; however, the same people say that customer service is at an all time low. What do you think?

Hutson

Well, I think both are valid points. One conclusion I would make is that customer service training has certainly not reached a saturation point as yet. Until a company really gets where it needs to be, training need is going to be apparent. Dr. Peter Drucker said many years ago that the purpose of the business is to attract and retain customers. The attracting, of course, is addressed in the sales and marketing side of a company's strategy. The retaining of customers is addressed in the issue of customer service. I look at it like this, David. Today all the weaklings in the market place are gone. They've already failed. Those people have moved on. Those organizations no longer exist. The only remaining companies out there in the market place for the most part are those that are already doing a fine job and they are working diligently to keep doing better. But the essence of that is an interesting result. The bar of excellence is going up on everybody. I happen to think that customer service is one of the greatest ways we can get over that bar, retain our customers, and go to the next level.

Wright

So you're saying the customers' expectations are higher?

Hutson

Absolutely, and I think a lot of companies are doing poor jobs of managing those expectations, and they need to work better on that as an internal part of their success plan.

Wright

It seems to me that customer service should be a manifestation of simple kindness, a respect for human beings, not to mention the fact that it's just good business. Am I just being naive?

Hutson

I don't think so. I agree with you. I think you've stated a basic truth here. There are no good excuses as to why it's not working like it should. I just believe as a natural thing, joy and positiveness require less energy than stress and negativity. You'd think people would just naturally provide great service, but it's just not as natural as it should be. It just doesn't work that way.

Wright

I've been familiar with your training style for many years, and I know you give people great suggestions to enhance their business. Can you share with our readers some how-to's you give to your audiences to ensure better customer service and increase market share?

Hutson

Well, in our limited time and space here, I've got a couple of observations that I think could be meaningful. The great Italian philosopher, Pareto, had so many great ideas. One was called Pareto's Law, which is essentially the 80/20 rule we've all heard about for years. One application of that to business as we know it today is that in most organizations, 80% of their business is derived from the 20% largest and most loyal customers. I have what I call Don Hutson's corollary to Pareto's Law. It takes it one more step. I think 65% of a company's business is usually derived from the largest, most loyal 10% of their customer base. So I think we need to always work diligently on the sales and the service side to avoid customer turnover and to keep these people excited about doing business with us. One way we can do that is perform some customer service miracles. I define a customer service miracle as anything we can do to make a customer say "WOW." When they say "WOW," they are talking to people out in the marketplace and our reputation begins to spread like a prairie fire on a windy day in a very positive way. Now, what is required to perform customer service miracles? I think we only need two prerequisites, a good heart, which means that we've got to want to perform miracles. It's got to be a part of our intent, a diligent desire to serve, if you will. The second thing we need is a keen eye to be able to spot the miracle opportunities. We need to have our entire organization focused on looking for miracle opportunities, especially with the 10% from whom we get 65% of our business, because we can't afford any customer turnover there! It would be far too disastrous. Let's give all the greatest service that we possibly can, but in that 10% let's just perform the miracles as readily and as often as we can for them.

Wright

In your customer service presentations, you refer to internal and external customers. I've never heard it stated that way. What's the difference between the two?

Hutson

Well, there are actually four types of customers in our U.S. Learning Training Model. I will just give you all four. Number one is the "external customer," traditionally considered to be the company or individual who spends money with us. They are the people who are doing business with us on a daily basis. Then we have the "internal customer," and they is known as the team members. Everybody who works at Insight Publishing are all internal customers to each other. Everybody working at U.S. Learning are internal customers to each other. The basic premise is that we should treat each other not as an inconvenience in every day interactions, but as team members and internal customers. Then we have what's called the "paternal customer," and that's your boss. Just about everybody has a boss. I think it's incumbent upon every employee of an organization today to enthusiastically buy in to their boss's vision, and to publicly and privately state that they are buying in and to behave accordingly. You can't work for somebody and not buy in. That's an incongruence. It just doesn't fly. The fourth is what we call "fraternal customers." Fraternal customers are members of your personal and professional network. We hear much about networking today and the importance of it, and we can gain a lot from people who are members of our network. We just need to remember that we must give to, as well as get from, our fraternal customers as time goes by.

Wright

That's interesting! Let's talk about sales. Some of the most unlikely people I've known have turned out to be great sales people. Do you believe that there's a sales profile or can anyone who tries hard enough make it?

Hutson

Well, that's a good question. Here's the way I basically consider success in selling. I believe that skill times effort equals productivity.

Now let's break down on the skill side. We've got product knowledge. We've got sales knowledge, people skills, knowledge of the marketplace, and just all of the knowledge that we need to amass to be successful in a given selling situation. And all of those, I think, are very important. If there's a weak link in there anywhere, it's going to short-circuit the success process. So all of those are critical components of the skill side. Then on the effort side, we have such things as an individual's attitude, their work ethic, their discipline and motivation. Thoreau, years ago, defined motivation as the pull of anticipation and the push of discipline. If someone is truly motivated, they're going to have that work ethic. They're going to make some positive things happen. Also on the effort side is what we call team spirit, a desire to succeed, and a desire to serve other people. All of those fit into what is essentially the mental side, the decisions we make as to how much energy we're going to devote to our career. So skill times effort equals productivity.

Wright

I wanted to go back and ask you one more question about customer service and I hope we're not too far off the subject, because a good friend of yours told me a few days ago that the customer service starts with sales. In one of your most requested presentations, the title is, *How to Make and Keep Customers Happy,* you talk about several concepts that will make customer service better and prove valuable in gaining a competitive edge. Can you give our readers a *Reader's Digest* version?

Hutson

You want the quick and dirty version.

Wright

That's right.

Hutson

Yes, let me present it in this manner. There are seven simple behaviors, which we've all heard, and it almost sounds like over simplicity. But I submit that when these seven (or most of them) are used there's a collective affect that is very powerful. For example, eye contact, when we communicate with somebody, if we'll look in their eyes, we heighten the awareness of what's going on in that interaction, and there's a higher quality communications flow taking place.

Have you ever talked to someone who was presenting an idea to you, but they didn't look at you?

Wright

Oh yeah.

Hutson

You catch yourself saying not only do I question whether I believe this person or not, I don't even think he believes what he's saying! So eye contact is critical. Secondly, a kind word. You never know when somebody might really need a kind word. It's easy to give, and it can be very meaningful. Next, a sincere smile. Well, people say, "I'm pleasant enough. I smile often enough." Well, we need to probably smile and be even more pleasant than we usually are, and we need to express that through the facial expressions that are pleasing to the people we communicate with. Next is positive energy. Have you ever walked into a retail establishment and if you can find somebody to wait on you, they're not excited about doing it.

Wright

Right.

Hutson

It's a real turnoff. I want somebody to serve me with positive energy that brings some excitement to the experience. They're expressing that they're glad I'm shopping in their facility and they're pleased to be able to serve me. That positive energy is something that we tend to respond very favorably to. Now tied in with that is a can-do spirit. A lot of people say, "Oh, we don't have that" or "you're not going to be able to find what you're looking for," or they give you some negative response to a request. I think people should have a can-do spirit and get innovative and creative to solve customers' problems any time they can. Next, we should use a person's name when we're talking to them. We don't want to over use it, but we don't want to under use it either. Well a lot of people say, "I can remember faces, I just can't remember names." That's because we never get it in the first place. We need to concentrate on getting peoples' names and using those names appropriately. And finally, thank them. Thank them for their time. Thank them for their business. Thank them for the opportunity to be of service. Now, my point, David, is that most people are very easily and naturally two-for-seven, maybe three-for-seven in typical interaction. I say we should develop a habit of trying to be six-for-seven or seven-for-seven, and we're going to get greater results with people.

Wright

That's great advice. Well, as you said, it sounds simple, but when I've thought about myself, I don't always do all of this.

Hutson

That's right. It's easy to overlook several of those components.

Wright

In your high performance-selling program, you teach people to shorten the sales cycle. What do you mean by that?

Hutson

Well, first let's define the sales cycle. The sales cycle is the length of time that transpires from the initial contact between the sales person and perspective buyer on a given topic or product being presented until the order is secured. Most sales people do not keep up with their average length of sales cycle. I contend they should. If they keep up with the average length of their sales cycle, they focus on it, they think about it, and they internalize it, they're going to get energized about shortening that sales cycle. I'm convinced that greatness in selling is observed when we see that there are some people who can compress a tremendous amount of achievement into a given measurable time frame. The way most sales people are able to do that is doing a lot of seemingly near insignificant things very well and with great consistency. So that's the issue there. We need to try to shorten the sales cycle. It's based on the idea that our success in selling is determined by how many people we talk too and how good we are when we do. Now we need to talk to a lot of people and we need to be very good in our process of making those calls and our discovery skills in presenting solutions and gaining commitments.

Wright

Tell us about your approach to selling. I remember you advocating a system designed to categorize people so that you could treat them as they would like to be treated. Could you explain to us?

Hutson

Well, that's called the concept of behavioral styles. As we discussed previously, David, I had the opportunity to get into this business at a very early age. One of the benefits afforded me was the opportunity in the '70s to work closely with Dr. David Meryl, who created the Social Style Concept. That's the behavioral style grid with the model using the driver, expressive, analytical, and amiable descriptions. It's based on the idea that all of us, in terms of our usual behavior, are in one of those four categories. We all have strengths and we all have weaknesses. I like to clarify that there's no best place to be. Wherever you are is okay. So it is indeed, I'm okay, you're okay subject matter. So we're not trying to put people in boxes, some of which are good and some of which are bad. So there's a respect for the dignity and individuality of all people. But based on those differences, there's predictability about how people will respond to certain stimuli. For example, the drivers like to be dealt with efficiency. They don't want to sit and listen to 20 minutes of rapport building. That's a waste of time to the task-oriented driver. The expressives like to be given a stimulating presentation, one that is enthusiastic and keeps their attention throughout. The analyticals, who are the opposite of the expressives, aren't really looking for enthusiasm. They want factual data accurately presented. The amiable, which is the opposite of the driver, is interested in relationship orientation, rapport building, and they are not interested in getting to the bottom line any time soon. So you see how those are distinctly different styles?

Wright

Yes, absolutely.

Hutson

The best sales people out there not only are keenly aware of their own style and how they are impacting on other people, but they use the skill of adaptability. They adapt their style to get on target with the person they are talking too.

Wright

Since everyone loves to buy the things that they want or need, why is it that most people have a negative view of sales and sales people?

Hutson

I think it comes from some very old tapes. Stage one in the evolution of the profession of selling was the product pitch. The product pitch could best be personified by the snake oil salesman in the 1800s selling off the back of his covered wagon. He presented a product of questionable quality to a crowd he had never qualified with little or no concern for the result of any transaction that might take place. He made all the sales he could and promptly packed up his wagon and headed to the next town. Unfortunately, that stereotype has been very difficult to wipe out of the minds of people in today's society. I'm convinced today that the best salespeople are concerned about the needs of their clients. They work diligently to identify those needs. They also work to present viable solutions that are win-win in nature, and they are also striving to create some symbiotic competencies so that they will be difficult to replace as a resource to that customer.

Wright

When I was thinking about your snake oil salesman, I started considering all the television shows that I've seen where they depict salespeople as over-zealous and interested only in the money, and stupid. I remember W.K.R.P.; the advertising salesman there even wore plaid jackets and white-topped shoes.

Hutson

Yeah, terrible. He was an exaggeration of the worst of all stereotypes. Flamboyant, manipulative, excitable, and not particularly concerned about customer needs.

Wright

Right. Most of the people that I've seen in the past few years that are in the sales business are as professional or more professional than any I've ever seen in years past.

Hutson

Yeah, it's like the organizations who have not done a good job of serving their customers have perished. Similarly, salespeople who have not done a great job of attracting and retaining customers have also fallen by the wayside.

Wright

Relationship selling seems to be a new buzzword as I've read titles and table of contents in bookstores. How do you define relationship selling? Do you think it has replaced the older methods of selling?

Hutson

Well, I think relationship selling was the first significant step to get us away from the stereotype of the peddler and the pitchman of years ago. I saw relationship selling emerge in the early to mid-70s, and it was like a breath of spring in the entire marketplace. Salespeople who did not embrace it quickly enough found themselves suffering and losing a lot of market share. I think it's as important today as it was back then. In the developing of positive relationships, there's an inherent understanding of the principle of getting inside a customer's head and finding out what they think and how they feel and where they're coming from. And that's a very admirable thing to do. It takes time, energy, and expertise, but when you do that, you are developing a positive long-term relationship that so often works for years and years.

Wright

You know one of the most surprising things to me about sales—I've been in the sales industry for many, many years—as I look at most of my close friends, my long-term friendships, that many, many of them have come from my clients. So I guess I was doing relationship selling and not knowing it.

Hutson

I think you were.

Wright

Don, I remember that you graduated from the University of Memphis with a degree in sales. In fact, I don't remember any other schools that offered a degree in sales. When you consider sales and service as a career, what advice can you give our readers that are considering sales as a vocation?

Hutson

Well, David, I think sales and service go hand in hand. I've never seen a great salesperson that did not have a strong spirit of service to others, and I've never seen a really good customer service person that didn't have at least some sales skills. So I think there's an overlap, and I think philosophically an organization today needs to consider that sales and service really do go hand in hand, and there's got to be a great deal of expertise in both arenas.

Wright

Are there colleges now that are giving degrees in sales?

Hutson

Well, I think there might be one or two and that's about it.

Wright

Why do you think that is?

Hutson

I think the stereotype we discussed earlier still lives. You see there are so many companies that try to come up with esoteric titles for their salespeople that do not have the word "sales" in them...

Wright

Right.

Hutson

... Like product engineer or account executive, anything as long as the word "sales" is not in it. I'd like to think we've turned the corner on that and hopefully will be enhancing the overall view of what selling is all about and how important it is in our marketplace.

Wright

I hate to even talk about statistics, but I read this many years ago. They said something about college graduates, out of the college graduates in that given year, the probability of the graduate going into sales was something like 5% or 10%. And then 10 years later of those same people, 80% of them were involved either directly or indirectly in some sales activities.

Hutson

Right. Which speaks to the undesirability of being any part of the profession as meets the eye because of the way it's been presented and because of the stereotypical impressions. But it also speaks to the importance of selling in an organization. You know what's the first thing that's on a financial statement? Well, on a basic financial statement on the top line is total revenue and that's sales. That's important. And any organization that doesn't have a good top line is going to have a real struggle having a good bottom line. So sales are what it's about, but service is what keeps the sales coming in.

Wright

Well it has been a great conversation. I've learned a lot. As a matter of fact I'm going to take four or five of these questions and answers that you've given me back to my staff and play them at the staff meeting, if you'll give me that right?

Hutson

Absolutely. I hope you can get some mileage out of it.

Wright

I really appreciate the conversation that we've had today and I wish you all the best as you go on in your speaking business and writing business. It's just really good to talk to you.

Hutson

David, it was my pleasure. I appreciate it.

About The Author

Audiences are captivated and entertained by Don Huston's personal anecdotes, used to drive home the business solutions he offers in his presentations. Participants leave each of his presentations on-track and focused, with new skills, attitudes, and ideas that work at the "street level." Don empowers audience members with the skills and cutting edge strategies needed to succeed in today's business environment.

Don Hutson

U.S. Learning, Inc.

P.O. Box 172181

Memphis, Tennessee 38187

Phone: 901.767.0000

Email: Don@DonHutson.com

www.donhutson.com

Chapter 7

KEN EDMUNDSON

THE INTERVIEW

David E. Wright (Wright)

If you are a CEO or business owner that struggles constantly with an underachieving sales force, and you labor over why your sales management is not fixing the problem, there is a simple, but powerful solution every CEO should know in order to dramatically turn the tide....you might be surprised at the powerful, hard hitting, no non-sense approach Ken takes in revealing his <u>4 Laws of the Overachieving Sales Organization</u>... 4 things that the top 5% of high-achieving sales organizations do which separates them from the rest of the pack. Ken, welcome to *Conversations on Customer Service and Sales*.

Ken Edmundson (Edmundson)

Thank you, David.

Wright

Ken, this topic should draw a lot of interest.

Edmundson

I get that response often, and although this is a huge problem in so many companies, it is really incredibly simple to resolve.

Wright

Where did you learn this?

Edmundson

I discovered it through failure! After many years of failure and frustration of hiring sales people only to see them drastically under-achieve their goals and my expectations it became a passion of mine to find a solution that worked. The vast majority of us who tend to the role of sales manager, CEO or business owners are not capable at determining whether a person actually has what it takes to succeed in selling. We hire people using the typical interview and background check techniques, or we watch our existing sales staff and assume the person that sells the most is our best sales person and we try to hire someone like them. There were 3 questions that always haunted me as a CEO and sales manager: 1) Why do we hire so many people that do not measure up to what we expected? 2) Are my top sales producers really achieving their maximum potential? 3) Are there core competencies that separate the over achievers from the rest, and if so what are they?

I began my serious research and study around a question that haunted me, "are some people just born with a natural talent to sell or can a person actually be trained to sell if they have certain key core competencies? If you ask the majority of sales managers they would tell you the most important thing in hiring good sales people is to find those people that appear to be natural born sales people or have sold successfully in the past... today I would tell you that is a formula for repeated failure... it simply means they look for people that: A) they like, B) have wonderful personalities, C) interview well, and D) have sold successfully in the past.

One of he most dysfunctional tasks of most sales organizations is how they hire their sales people or how they evaluate their existing ones. I've often said that instead of all the "unlawful termination" suits that exist, perhaps there should also be some legal action for "unlawful hires"....you know, those that should have never been made in the first place.

Wright

Do you believe selling is a natural talent or a learned ability?

Edmundson

Selling is primarily a learned ability... a skill you can acquire and improve... and the key here is "improve." If a person has certain key core competencies then they can absolutely learn to sell more effectively. A sales manager will fail consistently if they look for people they believe are natural born salespeople and do not understand how to select sales people based on their having certain key core competencies.

Wright

That's interesting. What do you mean?

Edmundson

Like many people I spent years building sales organizations myself and battling the frustrating task of interviewing and attempting to find, hire, retain and motivate good salespeople. I finally came to the realization that successful salespeople do not fit one particular personality type or model... one size does not fit all! They come in all shapes and sizes, all personalities and all genders. After years of trying numerous interview and hiring methods, I fell victim to the same myth that so many CEOs and sales managers believe, that 'good salespeople are *born* and not *made*.' How many times have we heard the remark, "They were born to sell"... it's a myth and if you continue to look only for salespeople that are "born salespeople," you will fail regularly! Most of us who have been in a position over the years to hire salespeople fall into the trap of doing it the way it's always been done. What people often mistake for a perceived "natural ability to sell" is really either, a personality they like, or in certain cases there does exist in that person a genuine interest and excitement to sell, and more than likely they do have some of the key core competencies we should be looking for, but the management team does not know how to measure for them and the sales person is not aware they exist and certainly does not know how to take advantage of them to enhance those strengths and overcome the weaknesses. This is different from having a natural born ability to sell, the core competencies can vary in which ones you have and the degree to which they are affecting you in a positive or negative manner. People actually learn these competencies somewhere in their life or work experience, they have

95

not existed their entire life. It is something we learn, but recognizing them and then using them to your advantage is the real power.

Wright

So you believe salespeople are made and not born?

Edmundson

Yes, but if you are skeptical about this idea, be open-minded for a moment and read some of the evidence we present. First, if you are tasked with the responsibility of building a sales force and you attempt to find only salespeople that are natural born salespeople or have had some success in the past, you will fail a majority of the time. 95% of the working population exists in some type of employment responsibility that requires interaction with other people, which is basically sales in some shape or form. They might call it business development, customer service, client retention or professional services, but at the end of the day, every company's survival is dependent on generating revenue and that revenue comes from some sort of selling activity by its employees... regardless of what title you give them. If you ask CEOs to describe the type of business they are in, 99% of them will describe their product, the clients they serve, or the service they provide. But, in reality, every company survives solely on their ability to produce revenue (sales); law firms, banks, CPA firms, hospitals, engineering firms or manufacturing companies... it's all about selling. I often hear CEOs say, *"If we don't get our sales up, we are in trouble."* But I have never heard one say, *"Our sales are going through the roof, we are setting new records in sales every month, but we are in real danger of going out of business"*... just doesn't work that way. Sales create the momentum and energy in every organization; it is impractical to think we can hire 100% of our salespeople who are natural born salespeople.

Wright

You've got a point. Are you saying anyone can learn to sell regardless of their personality?

Edmundson

No, I would be more conservative than to say "anyone," but give me a person who has a real passion, interest and desire to sell and that person can be trained to be incredibly effective in sales. The fact that a person is outgoing (extrovert) provides absolutely no assurance they will be successful in a sales career. An introvert can be just as successful in selling as anyone because they tend to listen, ask questions and process information better, which are critical skills in selling successfully. And this issue of wanting (having a passion) to sell is no small point. About 70% of the people that we test at our institute indicate they don't enjoy selling and most of them don't enjoy selling because it is such a battle for them on a daily basis and they find it to difficult to work in a market for which they are untrained. If they had been properly trained it would be easier and therefore a lot more fun. I don't know of a profession in the world that ends up with more people participating in it than the sales profession that didn't choose that profession... the profession chose them. In other words, people simply end up in sales because they didn't know where else to go, and yet many sales managers expect those people to enjoy it and like it without any real training. If your organization does not have a very targeted and specific, mandated, results-oriented sales training program, it cannot reach its upside potential, but it is likely that it will reach its downside potential.

Wright

I suspect this will encourage many CEOs and Sales Managers to know there are potentially many capable sales people in the marketplace, but how do you know which ones can actually become one of those high achievers?

Edmundson

The question I get asked by CEOs and sales managers most often these days, is whether there is some magic formula to determine if a person can really be successful in selling! In other words, they want to know how do they find the top achievers and eliminate all these underachieving sales people on their sales team, and the constant hiring mistakes from their sales force? This is where my **4 Laws of the Overachieving Sales Organizations** come into play full force...there are 4 things the top 5% of sales organizations do that others do not understand or cannot perform consistently.

The majority of companies fail to consistently achieve their sales goals for 4 simple reasons... these are the laws that are the most successful sales organizations live by constantly:

Law # 1) They recruit, hire and retain people on their staff that have the key core competencies required to succeed consistently.

97

Law # 2) Their sales people enjoy selling because they have been properly trained.

Law # 3) Accountability is correctly applied.

Law #4) Management accurately understands the goals and motivations of its sales people.

All 4 of these must be addressed if you want to build a powerful sales force that routinely overachieves.

Wright

Can you expound on each of these more?

Edmundson

Sure. Lets take them briefly one at a time.

Law #1) Recruit, hire and retain people that have the key core competencies to consistently and regularly succeed.

Most companies attempt to hire people they feel are "natural salespeople" or who appear to have "sold successfully in the past," and although you will find some success in that process it will not produce the constant results you want.

"A critical part of the secret to building an overachieving sales force is to learn how to test your sales people, and then become fanatical about testing them to determine if they have the key core competencies that make up the best sales people in the world."

A very small majority of sales managers actually know how to use the tools that exist in the marketplace to test their people and determine if they have the necessary competencies to succeed. There are some wonderfully powerful, effective assessment tools that can help determine those competencies. Tools that will tell you the behavior, the personality, the competencies that a person has to determine if they will actually execute in a competitive market on a consistent basis. If your sales manager is not competent in using these tools and applying them then you are using, at best, an educated guess to determine one of the most important aspects of your company's success.

The first law in building a sales force that will over achieve is to stop trying to guess at who can sell, while people are not natural born sales people, they do have certain core competencies which they have acquired or developed and are unique, specific and powerful key competencies which lend themselves to being more successful in selling. In reality no one can predict with any high degree of accuracy whether someone will fit into their organization and able to sell effectively by just using the typical interview process. Mathematically we have a 52% chance of hiring the right person if we just flip a coin, and studies reveal that we only increase that a whopping 8% by using our wonderful interviewing skills. Looking at someone's historical record can be a very misleading indication of whether they can continue that success, or if they are even achieving their maximum potential. No one ever sent out a resume, or suggested in an interview that they were not an overwhelming success in the past. I've never interviewed a sales candidate that told me anything but how wonderful they had performed in the past... makes you wonder how in the world their previous employer could possibly have let them get away. When looking at a salesperson's historical success, we don't have all the key facts about how or why that person became successful, if in fact they really did. And candidly, most sales managers don't know how truly verify the candidate's previous success anyway; they simply believe it when they see it on paper.

Wright

So what are these competencies you should look for that will help make the determination as to whether someone can consistently overachieve?

Edmundson

There are 7 basic competencies which must exist for a sales person consistently achieve at the highest level.

1) **PASSION** is the most important element for determining whether or not an individual has potential for growth. It is extremely difficult to motivate people that either lack or no longer have the passion necessary for greater success. Someone who is committed but lacks passion means their "bar" is lower than yours or mine. They are committed to reaching their goals, but their goals aren't as grand as yours or mine. Goal setting is the most effective way of increasing passion, even when it means starting the goal setting process over again. When someone admits to having a lack of passion, it is almost like they are saying, "Yeah, I don't care that much about being more successful."

2) **DETERMINATION** is the full, unconditional means to doing whatever it takes to succeed no matter what! Most people believe that their determination is quite strong. The problem we discover most of the time is one of conditional commitment. This means they are committed... but only as long as it is not too difficult or scary, without any discomfort or disagreement in principle in what they must do.

Sometimes lack of commitment is a problem because people don't have anything to which they can commit.

3) **SELF-DISCIPLINE**. The willingness to take the responsibility for your results. When people make excuses, they are actually selling themselves short. When managers accept their excuse, they are selling them short because they will find it even easier to use the same excuse again. It is important to know that real growth and change cannot occur until an individual stops making excuses and creates the self discipline to take full responsibility for their weaknesses, mistakes and results.

4) **ATTITUDE** is the most variable element for a person's success. Any person can develop an attitude problem on any particular day. It is important to discover the underlying cause, especially when the problem is a chronic one. When people have an attitude problem, they need to be monitored more closely than usual. The situation can easily change either by dramatically improving or worsening. An attitude problem has a negative impact on their bravery, therefore causing them to be very ineffective during the moments when they must be strong.

5) **SELF ESTEEM** People with well developed, high self esteem will be able to work much more effectively. They get business closed without the burden of worrying constantly about how they are perceived or valued by others. They will ask tough, needed questions without fear of upsetting prospects. They tend to not waste time with prospects that are wishy-washy and non-committal. They are less likely to take put offs and stalls in their selling.

6) **BELIEF SYSTEM** Every sales person in the world has a "belief system" those things they really believe are right or wrong with the selling process. Regardless of what the sales management or company policies are, ultimately under pressure every sales person reverts to their belief system when selling. People with a strong, well developed and correct belief system will be easier to train and will achieve constantly higher results. Any company can change their results temporarily by just changing the compensation structure, you can change behavior by changing by changing your accountability process and that works for a short period of time, but to change long term results you must understand and change the ineffective beliefs of a sales person.

7) **COMMUNICATION SKILLS** This covers a multitude of powerful issues. Overachievers are high learners! These are the things about communication they have learned: A) how to build trust-the foundation of any lasting relationship, B) how to ask questions for greater understanding not to trap people, C) how to listen with intense focus, as someone said, learn to listen with the same focus and intensity that we speak.

Give me a room full of men and women who have the PASSION, DETERMINATION, SELF-DISCIPLINE (no excuses), with a positive ATTITUDE (good self-image), HIGH SELF ESTEEM, STRONG SALES BELIEF SYSTEM AND COMMUNICATION SKILLS and I don't care how little sales knowledge they might actually possess, I will win with them every time over untrained, uncommitted, sales people who happen to have this "mythical natural talent" for selling. I know of no other profession where it is more true than in the selling world. *[bibliography #4-information developed by David Kurlan Objective Management Group]*

Wright

But how do you know if someone has these core competencies?

Edmundson

That is really fairly simple. There are some powerful and incredibly accurate assessment tools available to us today to determine what makes up this person that might become part of my all important sales team. Using and understanding assessment tools with your sales people is essential to make the first step to consistently over achieve. You can rely on them in targeting your hiring of new people or set up training to maximize your existing sales teams specific strengths and overcome their weaknesses. There are many effective assessment tools available, understanding which ones to use, how to connect them and how to interpret the results is a real skill. We found that the using a combination of different assessment tools to help us better understand a sales person's individual styles, strengths and weaknesses, and enhance their communication with those around them is a powerful learning experience, and creates a clear path for improvement for their training. We consider an assessment prior to determining whether someone could and should be hired or trained, the same as a doctor doing blood tests and x-rays before he declares you are sick or needs to have surgery....would you consider a doctor who just guessed? Assessments are your x-rays, and blood test, they will tell us if it is wasted money to train a certain individual because they don't have the essential core competencies for the training to actually work. Assessments should be done prior to hiring a sales person or training them. Companies that are not using them are committing what is equivalent to sales management malpractice. Using assessments will allow you to understand whether your sales team has the key competencies to compete at the top level.

Wright

Can you recommend some assessment tools you use?

Edmundson

Given the limited time and space we have for this chapter, I would rather reserve that for another time but if people will call me or contact us through our web site we will help them.

Law # 2) Over achieving companies train their people, it is the key to turning unhappy sales people into productive satisfied producers that stay with the company.

As you know, our study finally led us to develop a sales training institute... . we decided to put our money where our mouth was and prove that people can be trained to become over achieving salespeople. We really wanted to create a place where individuals who make their living by selling would have a place to go learn and actually improve in selling.

Our previous experience from running and building sales companies for 20+ years taught us a lot about the real need for focused and serious sales training and our experience certainly affects today how we train at our institute. At our training institute we are driven by our experience. High achieving sales organizations have serious, focused, consistent, long term reinforcement training. Research shows that companies that focus on training their people retain them longer with greater results.

Wright

What's the most important thing in a training program?

Edmundson

First, there needs to be a commitment by the leadership to a long-term change in the beliefs of their salespeople...this goes to one of the key core competencies we discussed earlier. The only way to change people effectively long-term is to change their belief system about certain sales issues. We tell our CEOs the only thing worse than training your people and risking them leaving, is not training them and having them stay.

Wright

How do you recommend a effective training program be designed?

Edmundson

An effective training program is designed similar to how medical and law schools train. Training should be designed to change belief; re-taping the poor beliefs you developed, getting rid of self-limiting habits which keep you from selling; putting the salesperson into as many actual practice sessions (role play situations) as possible, so they can prove that they have adapted the new beliefs and behaviors; give them lots and lots of practice sessions. Any training that is effective must include lots of practice sessions... we suggest any training program that is not doing practice sessions on camera is missing a powerful way to help reinforce the training.

Wright

How would you tell CEOs to evaluate the difference between effective training and ineffective training?

Edmundson

There is no magic formula, but here is something important to look for. Understand the difference between impact training and imprint training. Impact training is short-term. Imprint training is forever. An example of an impact would be, for example, if you ran your car into the wall and it was damaged, the car can be fixed . . . the impact was the temporary damage to the car. The imprint of that crash would be if the driver was seriously injured and had permanent brain damage that affected them the rest of their life. Impact is temporary and goes away shortly; imprint is permanent and changes the person or results forever!

Let's say you go on a wonderful vacation to a foreign country and fall in love with the country and its culture, you talk about it for a few months, you show pictures of it to everybody for a few weeks... that is an impact, but the imprint is when you move to that country and take up residence permanently. Imprint is permanent and changes the person or results forever!

Be sure when you select training that you know the difference. Set specific goals you want to achieve with your training... ask the trainer how they plan to create these changes in your sales people.

Wright

How would a company decide to hire a training company?

Edmundson

I am not sure they can decide how to hire a good training company without some help. It should be a process where the company CEO and the training company should decide together; a good trainer should only be interested in training people who are very serious about change and about becoming better. Frankly, no amount of teaching or training can help someone who doesn't want to improve.

Wright

What type of people get the most benefit out of training?

Edmundson

People who come for the right reason.

Wright

And what is the right reason?

Edmundson

Basically, people are motivated to change for one of three reasons. There is only one of these reasons that we accept in determining if someone is right for training or will get the maximum benefit.

1) Fear... you work out of fear and change because you are afraid something bad will happen if you don't. Some companies in America today operate on a fear management mentality: we will fire you, we will not promote you, we will transfer you if you don't meet our goals . . . that is their methodology for managing. Ultimately, they have to do drastic things to continue to raise the bar. People who only change due to fear are not easy to train.

2) Incentive... pay me more, give me more, reward me more... and I will do more. People who typically operate in that type of environment are not easily trained.

3) Growth... the people who are your most dynamic salespeople and have the greatest desire to be trained are motivated by a growth incentive... sounds like this, "I want to get better, I want to know more." We call those people high learners with a low degree of brittleness. These types of people want to know more, they are willing to expand their horizons, they are willing to take in new information, they are willing to take risks, they are high learners as opposed to someone who is a low learner. A low learner doesn't mean they are bad people. It just means they have invested all they want in knowing what they know and they are not willing to open up to new ideas. We say those people have a high degree of brittleness... they break easily.

Law # 3) Accountability is correctly applied. Probably the best piece of advice I was ever given is a quote that is hanging in my office about accountability. *"You teach what you know, you reproduce what you are."* I tell CEOs they are getting exactly the results they deserve from their sales team. You demand more, ask more, teach more, show more, and you will get more. There is a saying that says a CEO or sales manager has 3 positions they can take with their sales team: A) train'em, B) tolerate'em, C) terminate'em.

So often under achieving sales companies take the last 2 positions. Over achieving sales organizations understand, implement and demand accountability for the key performance indicators of its sales people. Good accountability is not about punishing the weak, it is about rewarding, recognizing and saluting the success. Identify those key performance indicators you know that must be tracked and do it!

Law # 4) Management accurately understands the personal goals and motivations of its sales people

One of the most frequent blind spots we find in working with companies is their lack of understanding, or consideration of the importance of the goals and dreams of their sales people.....what really motivates them to higher achievement! There is an old axiom that goes like this, "people will crawl over broken glass to reach their goals but not your numbers"... management that consistently overachieves understands the power of this law.

Again, this is where the power of assessments can assist you. The secret to motivate anyone in the universe is to find out what they want and then to find out how to help them achieve their goals. Most managements spend 99% of their time pushing their sales team to reach the companies goals and to achieve the companies bottom line...you will get what you want when you have helped your sales team get what they want. And it makes accountability work more effortlessly.

Find a way to make their goals important and visible so they know it matters to you.

Boaz Rauchwerger, one of the great motivational thinkers and coaches of our time uses the following example, and it works. Decide on a dollar amount that is appropriately attractive for the person you wish to motivate... not to high or to low... lets say for example with a sales person making $150K per year you might use $30K dollars Sit down for a visit and tell them you are going to give them $30K dollars but there are a couple of rules that go with it. 1) They cannot give it away, 2) They cannot pay off debts, 3) They cannot invest it, 3) They must use to reward themselves.

The question you ask now is, "What would you do with it?" Tell them not to answer for 24 hours and then set a predetermined time the next day to meet and discuss their answer. The answer they give you will be an incredible insight to what motivates them. Now armed with this information go forth and find a way to help them achieve this goal. I'll guarantee you for them to accomplish this goal they will find a way to help you accomplish yours because in order for them to achieve that which they most want, it will require them to raise the bar of performance and is that not what you are after anyway? Companies that over achieve place great importance on setting and understanding personal goals for their sales teams and then helping them exceed those goals. If your company is passionate about goal setting, but does not understand how, or is not skilled at doing so, then strive to learn more, there is massive amounts of excellent information on goal setting available in the marketplace. Again, time does not allow us to go into detail on this portion but if you contact us we will help you.

Wright

What are the most common problems you hear from CEOs about their sales forces?

Edmundson

The most common hot buttons I hear from CEOs and sales managers are things like:

"We are disappointed with the low closing ratio we have and the loss of market share we are seeing."

"We are frustrated about our inability to identify, hire and retain good salespeople."

"We are tired of selling nothing but the lowest price."

"Our salespeople seem to have a lower desire and commitment level than we need them to have."

"We are fed up with no prospecting from our salespeople and, worst of all, we are tired of seeing the pipeline full of things that never close."

"Prospects seem to control our salespeople."

"Our salespeople blame poor results on the economy, the company or other things they think are affecting them."

"We have no real defined system for selling."

Wright

Are those easy to fix?

Edmundson

Well, that depends.

Wright

Depends on what?

Edmundson

It depends on what kind of a culture the leadership wants to develop in the organization. Does the leadership want to develop a true sales culture or do they prefer a manufacturing culture, a technical culture, an engineering culture, or a financial culture in the company... they are all good models, but the strongest growth culture for an organization is a sales culture. Whatever the CEO is focused on, whatever the CEO is talking about, is what everyone in the company is talking about. Here is a short sales test I give CEOs: "Where would your organization be today if all the salespeople were just like you?" This will quickly tell you the type of culture that currently exists in the organization.

Wright

Wow! That will get underlined by a lot of salespeople and sent to their CEO.

Edmundson

Yep, usually does.

Wright

What are other questions you ask a CEO to learn how their sales force is functioning?

Edmundson

I can tell you a lot about a sales force by asking a CEO five questions:

1) *What is the turnover ratio of your sales force?*
2) *What is your accountability structure for your salespeople?*
3) *How do you compensate your salespeople?*
4) *How do you evaluate your prospect pipeline for new business?*
5) *How do you train your salespeople?*

Wright

What is one of the great secrets you teach salespeople?

Edmundson

Speed-reading! Salespeople need to read a lot of information. We all learned to read in school and that taught us to read in order to take a test. So we learn to read slowly to gather facts. Then we proceed later in life to read fiction, which has a story line and a plot and requires focus and attention. You can speed-read business books because there is generally one major theme and a couple of key points that you need to pick up. You can really avoid a lot of wasted time reading filler material. That is the reason I like the Insight publications because the authors are speaking directly and quickly to a major topic... no filler material.

Wright

In helping companies select salespeople with potential, what is your number one concern?

Edmundson

As mentioned earlier, most companies hire based on history and not on expected future performance. We look to hire salespeople whose assessments show that their desire and commitment give them the greatest potential to be trained, and that includes salespeople that are considered veterans in sales... the typical salesperson we train at our institute has 15 years experience. We want to gain an understanding of their true desire in working in sales and their commitment to do whatever it takes to get better. You would think that would be obvious in everyone, but it is amazing how often we eliminate people because they do not have the desire and commitment to proceed. Effective assessment tools are designed to help you have a keener understanding of the person.

In hiring salespeople, you want to ask yourself two questions: 1) Is the candidate I am thinking about hiring likely to be as good as my best people? And 2) *What are his or her key strengths and weaknesses and can I work with those effectively?*

The most expensive line item on our Profit & Loss statement that we pay the unemployed people that are still on our payroll. And on the flip side, we use two simple questions in determining if someone should continue with the organization. 1) *If I were starting over, would I fill that position? And 2) Would I fill the position with that person?*

If the answer to either of those is "no," then immediate action needs to be taken. Remember, "Your most expensive time is usually the time between deciding to act and when you actually take action."

Wright

In hiring people, what are some key rules you recommend to CEOs?

Edmundson

Other than doing the assessments to understand how to build a team with the strengths you want; there are a couple of recommendations. We find that most organizations do a fairly good job of interviewing, but they don't do a very good job of allowing the person to interview the company, so when they hire someone, they have a great understanding of their new salesperson, but then they realize that this person doesn't have a very good understanding of the company. Do "two-way interviewing" where the candidate and their significant other has a chance to really interview the company, set up an opportunity for them to spend a day in the organization, allow them to select people they would like to interview and meet within the organization. Another strong recommendation that seems to never fail, particularly when interviewing men who are married or have a significant other, is to go to lunch or dinner with them and allow the spouse or significant other to give you their thoughts about the person you are about to hire. It is absolutely amazing what wives will tell about their husbands and what you can learn about how they treat each other and talk to one another. Ask things like: 1) *What will happen when I call him at home late in the evening? 2) What did you like about all of his other jobs? What would you change about it? 3) What is the most important thing about him? 4) What are his business strengths and weaknesses?*

You will be amazed at how much information you will gain through this time with their spouse. Interestingly enough, it doesn't seem to work as well going the other way. If you are hiring a female, it doesn't seem to offer a lot of insight to interview the male counterpart. Men have gotten very good at playing the game, and they are not as willing to share and be open as we find the female companion is.

Wright

What do you find is the number one excuse for CEOs not wanting to make changes to their sales force?

Edmundson

They are afraid of making their sales force mad or losing them. Most CEOs don't do well with the unknown. *"They would rather be miserable than deal with the fear of the unknown."* But the best way to understand your sales organization is to try to change it. I am amazed at how many CEOs actually become frozen by a fear of change!

Wright

Of all the things you teach salespeople, what do you think is the most powerful?

Edmundson

You mean other than the fact that you can learn to sell? Other than that, I hear a lot of times that the most powerful thing they learn from us is how to set honest, realistic goals. Most people think they already know how to set goals, but they don't and, once we teach them, it changes how they approach their goals and it changes how management approaches their goals… it is overwhelmingly powerful. Effective goal setting will change how a person approaches his job

Wright

Do great salespeople know how to set goals?

Edmundson

All great people know how to set goals... great salespeople, great CEOs, great husbands, great wives know how to set goals... it's basic to what makes them successful. If a successful person reaches their success without setting goals, I'll guaranty they go even higher if they would learn to set goals.

Wright

Can you really determine in advance how effectively you can train a salesperson?

Edmundson

Sure, you now know about the core competencies to look for in a salesperson. Understanding each of those in your salespeople and how they are affected by their **"hidden strengths and weaknesses"** drastically alters how you train them and how quickly you get results. If we went into a great deal of detail here, we would be writing a book, rather than a chapter. But let me quickly add that throughout this interview we have mostly spoken to the issue of hiring new salespeople, I mostly work with sales managers and CEOs and dealing with their existing sales force. We look at the existing sales team much like we would if we were hiring them all over again, but without an interview. We test them and determine if their potential is greater than what we have seen or if perhaps they need to consider another opportunity somewhere else in the organization.

Wright

If you could only teach one thing to a salesperson, what would you teach them?

Edmundson

Oh, my... tough question. Probably if put under pressure, I would say we would teach them "Goal Setting," "Prospecting" or "Transactional Analysis."

Wright

That's surprising. I understand goals and prospecting, but why Transactional Analysis?

111

Edmundson

TA is a powerful tool for salespeople; it changes forever how people who know TA communicate. If people learn how to use this tool they will bring much more clarity into their lives. They will learn to communicate much more clearly with themselves and others than ever before. They will learn to assess people and situations much more accurately. They will take a lot of stress and emotions out of their business decisions, and they will make much more profitable decisions than they have ever made in the past. If they manage people, then they will grow more quickly. TA comes out of a marvelous and powerful study of psychiatry developed by Dr. Eric Berne, a noted California psychiatrist in the 50's. You might remember one of his popular books, "Games People Play." Dr. Berne died in 1970. TA is the study of the various ego states in which we all exist at any given time. I recommend any salesperson or executive learn as much about TA as they can possibly learn. Jut Meininger who has written some of the most defining works on TA in his earliest writings, *Success Through Transactional Analysis*, and his wonderful book called *How to Run Your Own Life*, is the real guru in TA. Jut has been instrumental in teaching us how TA applies in all areas of our lives; it is especially effective in selling. Steve Connor, who is one of the best executive TA coaches in the country, says 85% of all miscommunication is caused by our inability to understand and communicate correctly with the person in front of us because we are in conflicting ego states. All of us constantly exist in one of four ego states: 1) Parent, 2) Adapted Child, 3) Adult or 4) Natural Child.

Our Parent Ego State contains our entire "do's" and "don'ts", all the rules we live by. Our Parent tape is turned on at the moment of our birth and continues recording. You might recall Tom Harris described in his book, *I'm Okay, You're Okay*, that we have a huge collection of recordings in our brain of unquestioned or imposed external events perceived by a person from our early years. We always have that information to draw from. It's where we collect all of our intellectual data from everything that has ever happened to us. You have heard the statement that we are a collection of all of our experiences.

Our Adapted Child Ego State is basically a recording of our feelings and the emotions we experienced when we were exposed to certain events. It is a recording of what we felt when we lived through those experiences. It covers all of our fears and terror, feelings of inadequacy or pain. It houses all of the rebellious feelings of things we were forced to do. It also houses our guilt. In our Parent and Adapted Child Ego States we become judgers. Everything we hear or say is coming out of a judgment from our own experiences.

Our Adult Ego State is simply the computer in our brain. It is the unemotional fact gathering, non-judgmental part of our personality. It is where most of our clear questions come from. We often experience our Adult Ego State in sales when we are clearly asking questions to gain information. Salespeople often approach their prospects from their Adapted Child, a fear that they will not be able to sell them and the questions seem guided and appear to the prospect to be intended to trap them. Pure Adult questions, which come from a curiosity of interest in wanting to know, never hook the Adapted Child or Parent in the other person.

Our Natural Child Ego State is the real person inside of us. It represents the center of our personality. It is a source of intuition, joy, creativity, happiness, amazement, sexuality, desire and passion. It is where we daydream. It is where our aspirations are. It is where we like to play. It is the part of our personality that loves and trusts. It is the motivation behind everything we want to do.

Let me give you a simple TA example: a person says to me out of his Parent, "Can you believe how the modern teenager acts today? If I had acted that way when I was a kid, my parents would have killed me." I can now have a functional conversation because I recognized he is speaking to me from his Parent. I have a choice to speak from my Parent and say, "I agree with you. If I had acted that way when I was a kid, my parents would have locked me up." We are not having a very productive conversation, but it is functional. Our "Parents" are agreeing with one another. Or, I could speak from my Adapted Child and mumble to myself that sounds just like what my father or my mother used to say to me and I remember how much I hated it, and I could choose to say back to them, "You know, when you were a kid, the adults probably said the same thing about you. You probably acted the same way in your time." Now we have set up a dysfunctional conversation ready for battle because we are in different, opposing ego states. Or, I could take that same Parent comment and say from my Adult, "I wonder why they do that?" Or, I could say from my Natural Child, "Wouldn't it be fun to be a teenager again?" When a salesperson learns to observe their own ego state and how to exist in the most functional ones, they can have incredibly productive conversations with prospects. It is amazing to see your prospects gather information in their Adult, then make excuses in their Adapted Child, watch as their Parent requests more information, but it is their Natural Child that does the buying, that's where the excitement comes from to take action. Salespeople who learn this become powerful people. When we are able to teach our salespeople to literally live in the present without fear, the skills that we teach them can be incredibly powerful. *[bibliography #2, #3]*

Wright

How do you recommend people learn TA?

Edmundson

It is a process, first step, if someone is really interested is to read a couple of great books, Jut Meininger's *Success Through Transactional Analysis*, his marvelous book *How to Run Your Own Life*.

Wright

What is the greatest skill a salesperson needs?

Edmundson

The ability to listen, specifically to be able to listen to learn, not to respond. I refer to the listening a salesperson does with a client or prospect as the **"first silence,"** where you are paying 100% attention to what the person in front of you is telling you, be genuinely curious about what the other person is saying. The human mind has the capacity to process over 500 words a minute, yet most of us only speak at 140 words a minute, which gives the listener incredible capacity to think about other things, and most salespeople use that additional capacity to think about other things and not listen. So the first silence is listening to what is being said by the person in front of you. But there is another important silence good sales people observe. The other silence is what I call the **"second silence."** In fact, I am writing a book on that now. The second silence comes after the person speaking to you has stopped speaking and you literally pause a moment to think about what they said and how you will choose to respond. It's an incredibly powerful silence when learned to use appropriately. If you listen to a recording of most sales conversations, the salesperson rarely allows any silence in the conversation. It is like someone said, "in America communication is a competitive sport. The first person to breathe is declared the listener." In sales that is a death trap... silence solves more problems than words.

Wright

What is next on the list of important things to teach a salesperson?

Edmundson

Probably the second is the ability for salespeople to learn to sell at "eye level" or selling with an objective and not an agenda.

Wright

What do you mean by that?

Edmundson

Selling at eye level means believing that while you might not be peers with your prospect or client, you are equals. Teaching salespeople they can really help a prospect is important. If your salespeople do not really believe they can help a prospect, they are doomed already! Most salespeople do not believe that they have a product that can really solve their clients' problems.

We train our salespeople to be like "camels"... don't back up! A camel cannot back up easily; some experts will even tell you they cannot back up at all, but they certainly don't back up easily and if done incorrectly, it will break their back.

Wright

Why are salespeople so hesitant to sell at eye level?

Edmundson

Several reasons, but one is caused by what I call *"prospect rapture."*

Wright

What is prospect rapture?

Edmundson

It is when a salesperson that doesn't know how to prospect looks around and realizes he has only one prospect in his pipeline this month and you're it. He becomes nervous, he has no bravery, he won't ask the tough questions because you are his only prospect, and if you don't buy he is in trouble. Show me a salesperson that has a pipeline full of good prospects and I will show you a salesperson that will be braver, stronger, tougher and more successful because he sells from a different mindset. Prospecting is a major key for top salespeople. If your pipeline is full, you will sell with an objective rather than an agenda.

Wright

What do you mean by selling with an objective versus agenda?

Edmundson

People have a finely tuned sense when they are being sold. Most salespeople are trained to find out what the prospect needs and go for that need. They are taught to ask questions to get to the prospect's needs, but what they are trying to do is find out how to sell what they've got and to find out if they can develop facts from what the prospect tells them that meet their agenda, which is to sell what I've got! When a prospect senses that you have an agenda and are pushing to achieve that agenda, they will immediately begin to pull away. It's human nature. We train our people to sell with an objective. The objective is to truly find out from your prospect about their needs with no agenda. We train our salespeople to go to the prospect with a mindset that says, "I might not have anything that you need. I am the very best person in the country at finding out about your needs, and if your needs are consistent with what I sell, we might be able to do some business." How would you feel if you went to the doctor and he only had one procedure and one drug for all illnesses and when you walked into his office with a broken arm, he took x-rays of your stomach, provided a prescription for a stomach ache and turned you loose, you would say that was silly. When you enter the office of a physician, the first 15-20 minutes of conversation is all about what you feel, how long you felt that way, what hurts, where else does it hurt, how long has it been going on... the doctor wants to know everything he can know about what you are thinking and feeling because a good physician knows half the battle in getting you well is your believing in what he is about to recommend. It is the same thing with salespeople. Until your prospect trusts you and believes in you and that what you are recommending will solve his problem, no sale is going to take place. *[bibliography 2,3]*

Wright

What do you find the hardest thing to change in a salesperson?

Edmundson

Getting them to understand the difference between a problem and a fact of life. A problem is something you can do something about and should. A fact of life is something that cannot be changed, so stop worrying about it. A fact of life is what color your eyes are, how tall you are, what color you are. Stop worrying about it. Move on! Example, "It's the economy!" Common excuse we hear for poor performance. That is a fact of life... you cannot change it, so move on to something you can help like... more prospecting! The economy is a fact of life. Stop using it as an excuse. Other problems you can do something about. "I don't have goals," "I am not making the calls," "I don't have a good technique"... those are problems you can fix and should.

Wright

Where do salespeople waste the most time?

Edmundson

Probably not talking to the decision-makers. If you are not talking to someone who can write a check, you are basically wasting your time.

Wright

I know you don't like one-liners or quick fixes, but what advice would you give in closing?

Edmundson

1)"If a salesperson has a high need for approval, they are dead before they start... fix it quickly!"

2) "There is absolutely no acceptable reason to continually hire the wrong people or keep the wrong people in a job because you did not know how to fix it... there are ways to correct that problem."

3) "In today's business climate, you are required to eliminate that which is incapable of adapting."

Wright

I am curious then if you can learn to sell, why don't more people do it?

Edmundson

It seems fairly obvious. They really don't know they can get better, but mostly because they don't know where to go to get better. CEOs and sales managers are taught you must lead by example and that you really are not doing your job if you are only "coaching" your salespeople. For the most part sales managers use a system that says "watch me and do what I do," but they rarely have a system for coaching, mentoring and training their people to success. I strongly encourage CEOs and sales managers to learn to coach their salespeople or bring in someone who can. Training salespeople is like a good magic trick. The first time you see it, it looks impossible, but once you see how it is done, it is amazingly simple and you never forget it.

Here is a three-question self-assessment that CEOs can ask themselves to determine what needs to be done. *"Would I really be interested in: 1) dramatically improving my sales results?" 2) changing how my salespeople feel about selling and their sense of excitement about growing our revenue?" 3) improving how our prospects respond to us?"*

99% of CEOs and presidents will always say "yes." Now take each statement and ask these questions of yourself: *1) "Why am I interested?" 2) "What do I feel needs to be done?" 3) "When do I start?"*

Remember, the most expensive time a leader spends is that time between making a decision and actually implementing it. Your answer to these questions will tell you what you believe is wrong with your sales operation that needs to be corrected. Your job is to lead your company to a solution. Leadership doesn't occur when there is a mandate; we call that management. Leadership occurs when there is no mandate and you have to create one.

Wright

Back to the question we began with, do you believe anyone can be taught to sell better?

Edmundson

Absolutely, if they have a passion to do it!

Wright

Thank you for sharing your insights with us today on the subject of customer service and sales. I have learned a great deal, and I am sure our readers will too. Thank you, Ken.

Edmundson

Thank you, David.

Bibliography:

1. Sandler Sales Systems, Inc.
   10411 Stevenson Road
   Stevenson, MD 21153
   www.sandler.com

2. Jut Meininger
   Oklahoma City, OK

3. Synergy Development Associates
   Steve Connor
   675 Shadowridge Dr.
   Wildwood, MO. 63001

4. Objective Management Group
   David Kurlan
   182 Turnpike Road, Suite 209
   Westboro, MA 01581
   www.objectivemanagement.com

5. Target Training International
   16020 N. 77th Street
   Scottsdale, AZ 85260

6. Boaz Rauchwerger
   Boaz Power
   San Diego, CA.
   boaz@boazpower.com

About The Author

Ken Edmundson is founder, Chairman and CEO of the Edmundson Northstar Companies, parent company of Edmundson Northstar Training Institute, Edmundson Northstar Employee Assessment Institute and Edmundson Northstar Knowledge Institute. The firm is a recognized expert in training executional leadership, sales and sales management and customized employee assessment for companies across a multitude of industries.

Ken is also President and Managing Partner of Sparks-Edmundson Business Investment Group, a private investment partnership with interests past and present, in real estate, the marina industry, aviation, financial services and the Internet sector.

Ken began his career in 1975 with Martin Industries, Inc. of Alabama, a large privately held manufacturing firm with sales throughout the U.S. and Canada. At the age of 25, he assumed the responsibility as National Sales Manager and Product Director of a division with a 100-man sales force.

Ken's success in building large, service-driven, employee-motivated companies has led to his recognition as a prominent speaker, teacher and trainer on the subjects of "The Complete and Effective Salesperson," "The Honorable Way to Sell" and "The Perfect Employee."

In 1992, Ken was recognized by Memphis magazine as one of the top 100 Memphis business leaders who are contributing to the city and its growth.

Ken and his wife, Debbie, have been married for 32 years and are the parents of three girls. They work together in teaching and mentoring young married couples.

Ken W. Edmundson

Edmundson Northstar Companies LLC

Edmundson/Northstar Training Institute
is a Licensee of Sandler Systems, Inc.

775 Ridge Lake Blvd., Suite 160

Memphis, Tennessee 38120

Phone: 901.766.4560

Email: kedmundson@northstarinstitute.com

Chapter 8

PETER QUINONES

THE INTERVIEW

David E. Wright (Wright)

Today we are talking with Peter Quinones. Peter lives in New York and has many years of experience in sales, speaking, and training. His work has appeared in anthologies with giants of the speaking industry such as Les Brown and Warren Bennis. Recently, Peter has been developing a project for Industry Radio. Peter, welcome to *Conversations on Customer Service and Sales*!

Peter Quinones (Quinones)

Well, thank you, David. It's my pleasure to be here.

Wright

In one of your books you discuss "fusion," the idea of combining concepts that seem to be opposites. Can you give us an example of this from the world of sales?

Quinones

Sure! There are quite a few examples. I'll give you one example with a well known name—J. Douglas Edwards. Sometimes I'll be reading or listening to a program or at a live seminar and this name will come up, and it's always very interesting. A lot of people refer to his methods as something of the past that we can no longer use with today's customers, something from days gone by. Meanwhile, others are still advocating his methods, seeing them as still being very effective today. Plenty of trainers are still teaching Edwards' stuff in seminars. I think the truth lies somewhere in between, kind of following Aristotle's doctrine of the Golden Mean. So right here you have an example of fusion. Obviously with some customers, you can use certain methods and strategies. With others, they are not going to work. So I would say that in a case like this where you are aware of two opinions or two points of view regarding one person's famous (but old) techniques, to see what works and what doesn't in any given circumstance. I don't think everything is always so black and white. So that's one example of the principle of fusion in sales. Let's talk about another.

One time I was at a sales seminar and the speaker—a very well known speaker, by the way—told us if you get an assignment from a client and they are going to pay your expenses, always ask for a first class plane ticket. And he went on to give his reasons as to why that was a good idea. Similarly, I was at another seminar with another speaker, probably as equally well known, and he said, "Never ask your client to pay for a first class ticket, request a seat in coach." And he went on to explain his reasons for taking the economy ticket. Now both sets of reasons made a lot of sense. So here again was a situation in which two completely opposing viewpoints were being advocated by very well known people. And again, I don't think it's a cut and dried thing. I think it's something that has to be weighed on an individual basis.

Let me cite on final example, which I heard on audio training courses. A salesperson shows up for an appointment with a prospect and is told the prospect is in with someone else. He waits and waits and it grows to be over an hour over the appointed time. He scrawls a note on the back of his card, something like, "Hi, I'm here for our appointment, I see you're running late, but I'm waiting right here whenever you're done," and he asks the secretary to bring it in to him. The instructor of the course presented this as a nice technique. Now, on another course put out by the very same company, I heard another trainer refer to this very same incident and say the salesperson behaved like a scared rabbit!

Wright

I remember when I was younger, I used to respond to things like would the pink one be better or the blue one?

Quinones

Right.

Wright

Or would 10 o'clock be better than three?

Quinones

Exactly.

Wright

Now, I respond to people who are engaging me in conversation and not using those techniques so much. When someone says to me, "If I could show you the 'blank,' would there be any reason why you couldn't buy today."

Quinones

Right.

Wright

Then I'm thinking, uh oh, page 37 on the sales.

Quinones

You've heard it all, right?

Wright

But admittedly I've been in the sales business, like you, for many, many years so I don't know how other people respond. I do know that different people respond to different things. Over the past few years have you heard of any really new and exciting ideas or concepts in sales?

Quinones

Yes, I have. You know as we were just discussing, David, a lot of the old sales material goes over the same things—having a positive attitude, prospecting, presenting, addressing objections, closing, things like that. Most of the stuff you read is all about that kind of thing. A few years ago I worked with a brilliant copywriter named Joe

Vitale who introduced me to something that's really off the beaten path.

Wright

I know Joe.

Quinones

Oh you do!

Wright

Yes.

Quinones

Great. He introduced me to a concept that I found fascinating. It's called *Hidden Selling*, and I don't think that he himself made it up—I think he uncovered it in his research. In his book about P.T. Barnum he wrote about it in a way that anybody can understand. I can give you an example of what it is. He talks about a famous party that was held in New York in the Waldorf Astoria back in the 1920s, and it was called the Green Ball. If you were invited to this ball, you were required to wear green clothes—everything was green—the table cloths, the furniture, the food. You had to wear green when you went. People were giving lectures about the color green, why green has been so important in history and so on and so forth. And no one ever knew why this ball was given, who was behind it or what the purpose of it was. It turns out that a public relations man named Bérnays had staged it for a client of his who was very worried because their product was packaged in green, and it didn't seem to be selling very well. So they wanted to uplift the image of the color green and this was one of the strategies that Bernays used for them. Joe called it hidden selling because no one knew who was behind it.

I picked up on this strategy and I've applied it on one of my websites and am trying to develop a product by means of this method of hidden selling right now.

I'd also like to mention briefly a book by a gentleman named Michael Boylan called *The Power To Get In,* which is quite remarkable. It's not a sales book as such, but it's about gaining access to inaccessible people. It's totally original and will help any salesperson a lot.

Wright

In contrast, are there any principles in sales that are timeless and don't really need change much?

Quinones

Oh, absolutely. Does this sound familiar: " Find out what people want and help them get it."

Wright

Yes.

Quinones

That's from the book, *How I Raised Myself from Failure to Success in Selling*, by Frank Bettger, which was written, I believe, in the '30s. And to me this is really the only book any sales person ever needs to read. I think every concept that we study about in modern sales comes from this book. And one of the most important things that he talks about is being able to see things from your prospect's point of view rather than your own. Principles like these appear in different formulations in hundreds of books and articles about sales, and they all come from Bettger. I'll give you an example of a sales- person I once had who was completely unable to put this idea into play.

This was in a car dealership, and we were selling a small convertible to very wealthy people in a beach community. One day a young lady comes in with her father, she's about twenty years old, and she's looking at this convertible. Now this salesperson was a real motorhead, a technology geek . He could take a car apart and put it back together with his bare hands. So he assumed that this young lady would be interested in how the pistons fire in the cylinders, how the cable shifters work when you switch gears, the compression ratios, the intake manifold, things like that.

He had the hood of the car up and he was showing it to these people. And you know he's basically losing a sale because he's not talking about their interests at all. Their eyeballs were spinning. Being the manager, seeing he was losing them, I wandered over and said to her, "Well, aren't you going to look cool at the beach with the top down in this thing, blasting music, four of your friends with you, checking out all the cute guys?" Her father shrugged and just took out his checkbook because he saw that it was over. Her eyes brightened up like stars. So that's an example. You have to talk about *their* interests, what they're interested in. And I think that's one of the most time-less, ever present, principles of a sale.

Wright

So how important do you think customer service is in the overall sales environment today?

Quinones

Well, more and more I think it's perhaps going to become the major differentiator. I think the businesses that succeed are going to be successful due to their customer service strategies. And one of the great examples of this in our time is Nordstrom. You read things about people who are asked, "Which department store would you most like to shop in if you were given a choice?" And they say, "Nordstrom." And you find out later there's not even a Nordstrom in that town. But its reputation has preceded it to the point where people want to shop there. And I think that in that sense, it's very important. That's in a strictly economic sense. But I think it's also important in another sense. I think that when you give your customers good customer service, whether it's on a company level or on an individual level, it fulfills you. You take pride in your work. You have a belief that you're living your life correctly, that you're helping people and helping them get what they want. You're making them happy. You're helping them out with major purchases, perhaps a lot of money is involved, a lot of decision making, and you feel good about yourself because you know that you're not only doing business, but you're doing right by people. You're actually helping improve their lives. You're making a deep connection with them on a really fundamental level. I think that's one of the major benefits of customer service: it provides the salesperson with a great feeling of being of service to fellow human beings.

Wright

Early on in my life, I started selling real estate, and I really loved it. I sold it for years. Then I was making so much money it was almost embarrassing to my family, but my mother used to tell her friends that I had a sales job until I could get a real job. You know a lot of people seem to get into sales just for the sake of getting a job. What is the difference between this and entering sales with the intention of making it a career?

Quinones

Well, that was a great lead in to the question, David. I think that a lot of people—especially in today's times when maybe a lot of people are struggling, the economy isn't so great—just take a sales job for the sake of having a job, just so that they can say they're employed. And I think that salespeople in general still have this kind of image with the public of being snake oil types. As if you're doing something that's not quite ethical that has this stigma attached. And that's a mistake. I've sat side by side with salespeople who are actually in sales, doing a sales job, and they have that very attitude about what they were doing in sales. It's terrible. I can remember when I was a sales manager, if I put an ad in the paper for a salesperson, I would get maybe four or five responses. If I put an ad in for a porter, I would get seventy five responses.

Wright

Oh, goodness.

Quinones

Which shows you the attitude that people have toward sales. Also, I don't think that people quite appreciate the type of fulfilling career you can have in the sales profession. As you mentioned yourself, the opportunity to make money is just tremendous. But people would rather go for the so called steady paycheck or guaranteed income rather than choosing a career where they really have a chance to express their individuality and creativity as human beings and to make as much money as they want, all of which are opportunities that sales gives you.

Wright

Within the last three months I had one lady came into my office one day, and I was paying her $8.00 an hour. And she said, "I've been here a long time. I think you need to give me a raise." And I said, "Well, okay." And I said, "How much do you want?" She said, "Well, I think ten would be great." And so I said, "Did you check your W-2 last year?" She was making $18.00 an hour because of the bonuses. So I said, "Well, what do you want me to do? Do you want me to go ahead and raise you to ten and take the bonuses out?" And she actually said, "Well, I'd rather have the salary, the $10.00."

Quinones

Oh, boy.

Wright

So after I explained it to her you know then she saw the error of her ways. But a lot of people are just so negatively conditioned against commission sales.

Quinones

Oh, absolutely.

Wright

It's incredible! So what do you think is the greatest advantage of a career in sales in your opinion?

Quinones

Well, I would say there's two or three. The first one, I would say, is that you can actually study your subject. You'll never see a book about how to be a great clerk or how to be number one at pumping gas, but you can go to Barnes & Noble or you can go online and you'll see hundreds of books about sales. So there's an immense opportunity to improve yourself. There are innumerable audio programs, videos, and live courses that you can attend that can really help you improve. So if you have the desire to learn , the knowledge is definitely there to be had. That in itself should be indicative to people that hey, this is the type of career where you can make a lot of money. And that's the second advantage—the income opportunity, as you mentioned. Thirdly, I think that in sales you learn a lot of life skills, especially if you're selling a product that almost everyone has to buy, like real estate or cars or insurance because you meet people from all different walks of life. I mean I could tell you, and I'm sure most good salespeople can make a similar claim, no matter what you need done in this world, I've sold a car to somebody that does it. All these people are in my Rolodex and it makes life a lot easier. If you have a situation where you need advice, in any aspect of your life, you can just call one of your clients whom, over the years, you've developed into a friend. It is so much easier to go through life this way than cold calling everybody through every situation. So I think those are the three greatest advantages in a sales career. First, you can study and improve; second, the income opportunity; and third, meeting people and really creating a big , solid , life enhancing network.

Wright

I know you're probably a book...sales book freak and seminar attender like I am.

Quinones

Yes.

Wright

On the subject of sales, in my life at least, I love to go, but some of the people I would work with would say, "Oh, man, do we have to go to this sales conference today?" I would just leap in there and kiss the desk early in the morning because I found that almost everything that I learned in sales and in marketing helped me in other areas of my life more than they did in sales.

Quinones

Absolutely.

Wright

Because it was all communications and how to do things properly.

Quinones

Absolutely. It's not only sales *per se*, but you learn about all the areas of life. And I'll bet, David, in most of those cases, it was always the people who really needed to go that didn't want to go.

Wright

That's right. That's right, yeah. You know today's customers are more and more educated about the products that they want to buy, much more knowledgeable than they were in the past, and come to the sales process armed with research from the internet, et cetera. How has this affected the sales process and sales people?

Quinones

You know I think it's completely forced sales people to go in a different direction than they used to go in the past. And I think we're going to come to the point where customers are going to have dealer cost or supplier cost on virtually every item. They're going to know that the storekeeper paid $100.00 to Sony to buy this television, and they walk into the store and see it has a price tag of $319.00 on it, and they're going to go into this Priceline Dot Com mode. This is what happened in the car business about ten years ago. Costs, actual dealer costs, of cars were plastered all over the internet. People started walking in demanding to buy cars for just a few dollars over dealer cost. I think something like this is happening in real estate now, David, with these 1% commission guys?

Wright

Right.

Quinones

Yes, so most sales people would probably disagree, but I think this is actually a good thing, because I think it helps you bond with the customer more quickly, and build trust and rapport more quickly. I always say, "Great, we respect customers who do their research. You know what you want to pay. I know what I can sell the car for. It's just a very short conversation about negotiating a price now." Everything else is taken care of. In many cases these customers know more about the product than the salesperson does—they've done so much research. So I think this is the wave of the future. I think it's going to be happening in more and more industries. And I believe salespeople have to be flexible, accept this as the way it is, a fact of life, and gear the sales process more towards retaining this customer over a long period of time rather than just selling to them once, making a lot of money, and never seeing them again or trying to build long term relationships, get referrals, et cetera.

Wright

What's really scary is…I never thought I would do it, but the last three computers that I have purchased have been off the internet. And they delivered them the next day.

Quinones

See that?

Wright

I got more of what I wanted like a Chinese restaurant menu type choice…

Quinones

Right.

Wright

... and I didn't have to settle for less that what I wanted because they would just add anything I wanted to pay for.

Quinones

That's great.

Wright

And when they banged on my door the next day, I almost fell over. There's going to be a lot of competition like you said. Going back to customer service, what are some of the really important issues facing sales people today?

Quinones

Well David I think that customers are overwhelmed today. They're just bombarded with information, sales pitches, sales calls. I mean you yourself, sitting in your office, how many sales calls do you get a week?

Wright

Oh, my.

Quinones

It's crazy. I think that customers now want a quick, fast, and honest sales process. And I think that sales people and companies that are able to communicate this with people are going to be the winners in the business environment of the future. And I think the only way to do this is through customer service, through word of mouth, testimonials, and demonstrating to your customers that you're going to take care of them over the course of time. I think you have to really want to go out of your way to delight your customers. We have an insurance company here in New York, and when they pick up the phone they say, "How may we delight you today?"

Wright

That's great!

Quinones

Which I think is the object of a transaction, to delight the customer. Some even go beyond delight and ascend into the realm of amazement—amazing the customers. There are certain cases where you want to amaze a customer and thereby win their business for life. We spoke earlier about Nordstrom. They're excellent at this. I think this is the way to go in the future. I think in the future most sales training is going to boil down to customer service training.

And if I may just comment on one last aspect—diversity. It is so important, especially in retail, in large cities, to have bilingual salespeople. Without getting bogged down in political debates about it, it's just smart business sense and a tool to help capture more customers.

Wright

I've always thought, at least the last 20 or 30 years, that helping people make decisions is the way I sell more readily than any other. For example, when you said while ago, there's not a book that says how to be a clerk? Well, from kindergarten all the way through college, I never walked through a door where the title of the class was decision making.

Quinones

Right.

Wright

And in fact, in my family and most of my friends that I've checked out in later years, the people who love us most protect us and keep us from making our own decisions.

Quinones

That's it, exactly.

Wright

What do you think salesmen do to really learn how to help people make decisions they are conditioned not to?

Quinones

Well, you know, David, one time I was spending a lot of money on electronics equipment, and the salesperson gave me a brief overview. Then he said, "If this is not the right equipment for you, I would prefer that you don't buy it." So he was right up front, open, honest, and very sincere. He did exactly what you are talking about. He helped me make a decision, which I appreciated. And I'm sure that guy does very, very well in his sales career. He deserves to. He *did* help me make the right decision. I eventually did buy from him, but he was extremely persuasive right up front. He told me the truth—he said this may not be the right equipment for me—in a situation where many salespeople would have just tried to get me to buy it. So that kind of sincerity and honesty, I think, is always rewarded—both monetarily and emotionally.

Wright

And price is not always the major factor, is it?

Quinones

No, absolutely not. No. I mean if you want to...you meet a new boy friend or girl friend and you want to impress them with dinner, you don't take them to McDonald's you know.

Wright

Right. Let me write that down if I ever start dating again. The phrase "high tech high touch" surfaces a lot in sales literature. What does it mean, and especially in today's world?

Quinones

Well, I'll give you an example, David, of high tech low touch. Let's say I've been drinking Coca Cola my whole life, but one day I wake up, I go to the supermarket and I buy a six pack of Pepsi. You think down in Atlanta at Coke headquarters there they're saying, "Hmmm, let's get someone over to his house and find out why he switched"? This is high tech but it's no touch at all. On the other hand, if I've leased a car to someone and in my records I see that their lease is up this month, I can call them and say, "Listen, your lease is up. Let's get together. Let's start talking about your next car and find out what we can do for you." So that's high touch, staying in touch with people. I used to work with a salesperson when I sold Volkswagen who had a great high touch idea. In the Volkswagen cars there is a little vase for a flower on the dashboard. Every month this guy would mail all of his customers a little plastic flower, the flower of the month, to have in their car. Now you could imagine the amount of referrals this guy got just from doing a silly thing like this. But he was very high touch, very personal, and it earned him a lot of business. So I definitely think the way to go in today's environment is through the personal touch because it helps you differentiate yourself from all the yadda yadda yadda that's out there.

Wright

I do business with this lady who lives up in Maine. And a few months ago she called me and we were having just a conversation about her book that I had published for her and how we were going to market it and all. And I said, "Well, what have you been doing lately?" And she'd been gathering up oysters outside in the bay right out of her house you know.

Quinones

Oh, wow!

Wright

And so I said, "Oh, man that sounds great!" She said nothing else about it. The next morning I got an ice pack Federal Express, and I opened it up; you would have thought she'd sent me a Jaguar.

Quinones

There you go!

Wright

It was wonderful!

Quinones

Oh, that's a beautiful example. Let me write that down.

Wright

I also had a friend that when somebody would give him a referral, he would send their wives a letter of thanks, not the person that referred, but his wife.

Quinones

Wow!

Wright

He would go to the bank and get five brand new twenties and he would put them in the letter so that when she opened the letter the twenties fell out in her lap.

Quinones

My goodness. Wow!

Wright

The visual image of that he said, "My referrals have quadrupled."

Quinones

I bet. That's a great strategy.

Wright

What's in the future for you as far as sales training is concerned? What are you doing now?

Quinones

Well, right now I'm working with a company called Industry Radio trying to get some commentaries on a couple of their programs and it's in very preliminary stages, but hopefully someday we might have a radio program about motivation and sales training, some of the things we've been talking about today.

Wright

So it would be available over the internet then?

Quinones

Oh, absolutely. Yes.

Wright

Well, great. Well, Peter, it's always a pleasure talking to you.

Quinones

Thank you, David.

Wright

I always have so much fun that I guess is the reason why I always learn so much.

Quinones

Boy, I learn a lot from you too, believe me.

Wright

Your experiences are just unbelievable. I remember listening to you in a presentation one time. I sat there with my mouth open. I said, "Where does this guy learn all of this stuff?" I thought I'd just come up to your house up there in New York and spend a week with you just to take in some of this knowledge that you've got.

Quinones

I 'd learn more from you than you would from me, David.

Wright

Today we have been talking with Peter Quinones. Peter lives in New York and has years of experience in the sales business. And I can testify to his speaking and training ability. He's just a marvelous, marvelous speaker. Peter, we really appreciate you being with us today and taking this much time out of your morning for *Conversations on Customer Service and Sales*.

Quinones

Oh, it's my pleasure to be with you, David. Thanks for having me.

About The Author

Peter Quinones lives in New York and is the author of several books, most recently, *The Dream Factory*. Peter is currently developing a potential project for Industry Radio.

Peter Quinones

PO Box 478

Brooklyn, New York 11209

Phone: 917.941.2387

www.PETERQ.NET

Chapter 9

JIM CATHCART

THE INTERVIEW

David E. Wright (Wright)

Today we're talking to Jim Cathcart. Jim is a specialist in human development. He has been a corporate executive, a training director, entrepreneur, psychological researcher, meeting planner and association executive. Jim Cathcart is one of only five speakers in the world who hold the following honors: President of the National Speaker's Association, the Speaker's Hall of Fame, Certified Speaking Professional and a winner of the Cavat Award. In 2001, he received the Golden Gavel Award. Jim is also a member of the exclusive Speaker's Roundtable, made up of 20 of the most popular speakers in the world. Among professional speakers worldwide, Jim Cathcart is a leader. He has risen to the top of his profession through more than 27 years of speaking and training before 2,000 audiences in virtually every discipline. His client lists include ASAE, Motorola, MassMutual, Prudential, Northwest Bank, Becton Dickinson, Microsoft, John Deere, Levi Strauss, the United States Airforce and hundreds more of the world's top organizations. Author of relationship selling and 12 other books, Jim has also created over 70 video programs. Jim Cathcart, welcome to *Conversations on Customer Service and Sales*.

Jim Cathcart (Cathcart)
Thank you, David. It's nice to be on the program.

Wright
Jim, there's probably been more information given in workshops and seminars, books and audio cassettes, CDs and videos on the topic of customer service than any other topic. When I talk to most people, customer service seems to be at an all-time low. Why do you think that is?

Cathcart
I think it's probably not so. I think it's a matter of perception rather than reality. Let me explain what I mean by that. Years and years ago, we were small communities. You know, when the United States wasn't as urban as it is today. People knew each other and so, naturally, service was more direct and more personal and it felt more sincere. You always knew where someone lived in case they didn't stand behind their product you could go by their house and say, "You want to rethink that?"

Well, today there are so many of us and our society is so urban that even though we're hyper-connected with all of the communication devices and television and everything else, we don't feel the kind of personal connection with people, as a rule, that we felt back then when we were closer in smaller communities and people didn't travel that much. Look at the amount of travel people do today. It's enormous compared to when I was growing up, for example. When I was growing up if somebody had been to either coast—I grew up in Arkansas and if somebody had been to California or New York, it was unique. Well, today if you lived in Arkansas or Texas or anywhere in the middle of the country and someone hadn't been to California you'd say, "Really? Why not?" So, the perception is very different.

All through the '80s and '90s we had an enormous "service orientation" that started as early as the book *In Search of Excellence* by Peters and Waterman. There was also another book called *Service America* that Ron Zemke and Karl Albrecht wrote. Those emphasized the concepts of customer service being really measured and implemented as precisely as something you would in a manufacturing setting. So, everybody came up with a new thing: "Customer service is our only business." "We care about our customers." "Customers first." You know, all these slogans. The Customer Service Index (CSI) was implemented within the automotive industry and completely revolutionized the way they were doing follow through and attention to detail. Lots of other industries did that. Then you started getting the Malcolm Baldridge Award for excellence in quality and service and so forth. So, our culture has had a rebirth all around customer service and it's part of a societal evolution, if you will. It is part of a much bigger thing that's going on. As a matter of fact, customer service in many places is exemplary. I mean it is over the top extraordinary. But we've become spoiled. We've become conditioned to expect customer service to be outstanding. So, if we just get ordinary service we feel offended by it and gripe and complain. "This guy didn't hold the door open for me," or "These guys didn't even send me a personal follow-up note." "Gosh, I went there the other day and their coffee was stale." What? They offered you coffee? You know, I mean, you start thinking about that and it's like my own experience this morning.

I had to take my car down to get a tire replaced and I though I was going to get it repaired. I had bought a fancy new car and found a nail in the tire the other night. I pulled the nail out and, of course, the tire hissed at me and went flat and I changed the tire. Then I went in—being spoiled by high-level customer service experiences, I expected the dealer to just replace the tire and make everything fine. They didn't. I had to buy a new tire. I said, "Did I have the road hazard warranty?" They said, "No, you chose not to get that when you bought the car." I said, "Oh, okay, so it's my responsibility." But my first reaction was to be kind of hurt and offended. "Well, gee, this is bad service." No, it's not. It was just bad luck. I got a nail in my tire. It happens to people all the time. So, I shouldn't expect—if I'm not buying the extended warranty or something—I shouldn't expect to have it fixed, but I did. When I realized and had my little "wake-up moment" and realized this wasn't covered I said, "Oh, okay. That's life." You roll with the punches and you get over it.

Wright

I grew up in a time, especially in restaurant service, where you sat down at a table and waited forever.

Cathcart

Oh, exactly.

Wright

I remember going to a Burger King recently with my 14-year-old daughter. This fellow in front of me ordered a #3, or whatever it was, so the lady said, "Here's your Whopper and Coke, it'll be three minutes on the fries." He said, "What?"

Cathcart

Three minutes? Oh my gosh. "I could build a house a three minutes, what are you telling me?" We get on the Internet and we look at our e-mail. If it takes an extra 30-seconds to come up we're saying, "Come on! Come on! Come on!"

Wright

I got broadband because of that!

Cathcart

Even with the latest high speed lines we get spoiled. Then sometimes if you're out and have to use a dial up modem you sit there and think, "Gosh, how did people ever stand this?" The answer is it's not something you have to stand, it's still a convenience. Two or three minutes is fast compared to most of the world.

Wright

Should common decency and respect for all people lead the way in every customer service program?

Cathcart

I think more than that it should lead the way in everyday life. Do you agree with that?

Wright

Yes.

Cathcart

That's one thing that we've got to remember. It's way too tempting to fall into the entitlement mentality and think, "I deserve better service. I demand that I be treated like a king or queen and if I don't get it I'm going to file a lawsuit." How absurd is that? What we've got to recognize is that all of us are trying to get through this life in the best way we can. We're trying to do as little harm as possible, have as good a time as possible, and experience as much love and satisfaction as possible. It takes a lot of figuring out to get to the point where we can do that on occasion. So, it really does make sense to cut some slack to other people and let them occasionally have a bad day without saying that they're no longer a worthy person. If your best friend has a bad day, you kind of roll with the punches and get over it. You expect that they will apologize sooner or later if they did something offensive, but, still, you let them get over it. If someone else on the street has a bad day you expect them to rot in prison for having had a bad day or something. We overreact way too much. I think we ought to lighten up in our expectations. But still, have high standards. Expect a lot from yourself. Expect a lot from the quality of the work you produce—whether you are in a service or product business. Expect a lot from your people. But understand that we're all human. Make allowances for that. It sure makes life a lot easier to tolerate.

Wright

I think one of the things that really pointed to customer service and all of the customer service workshops that I have attended down through the years. Fifteen or twenty years ago, everyone started coming out with these statistics about how much money it costs when you run someone away...

Cathcart

Oh, yeah. It's like five-times the cost to replace a customer than it is to keep a customer. Even if you're spending a little extra in serving them. Look at TARP (Technical Assistance Research Program). This was reported first, I saw, in the book *Service America* back in the '80s. It said that they did a study on customer service and they found that people who were satisfied, had a great service experience and left the place just feeling a glow because it was so wonderful would tell from five to nine people about this wonderful experience. Yet, people who had a bad experience would tell from 13 to 20 people about it.

So, somehow in human nature there is this tendency to want to share our horror stories rather than our success stories. If you understand that and look at dealing with customers, you realize that it doesn't make sense to quibble over a few dollars when you're talking about thousands of dollars of potential business. One of the lines that I use in one of my seminars on customer service—actually it's on relationship selling—I ask the audience, "If I have, as a customer of yours, if I have 40 years of buying lifetime, how much of that business do you want to get?" The answer, of course, is all 40 years of it. I say, "Okay. If you and I argue over a little detail today, what's the likelihood that you're going to get the next 39 years of business from me?"

Wright

Great question.

Cathcart

Yeah. I went into a motorcycle store one time to buy some gloves that were summertime riding gloves. I bought a cheap pair of $22 gloves, took them home, got them out of the package, put them on and they didn't feel quite right. So I took them back the next day and said to Scott, the guy who had sold them to me, "Scott, I'd like to exchange these gloves for this $1 cheaper pair of gloves that are out of the package because the cheaper ones fit me better and you can keep the dollar." He said, "Have you got a receipt?" I said, "Of course I've got a receipt, you gave it to me yesterday." He said, "I mean with you." I said, "No." He said, "Well, Jim, I can't exchange your gloves." I said, "Sure you can." He said, "Well, you could have stolen those." I said, "Scott, stop for a minute. Just stop and notice that you know who I am, you remember selling these to me and it's not really likely that I stole the gloves you remember selling to me yesterday." He said, "Well, that's true." I said, "But the reality here is that you don't have authority to give me a refund without a receipt, do you?" He said, "No, I don't." I said, "Then you could have started with that. But let me talk to your boss." So his boss came over and used one of these charming opening lines, "What's the problem here." I thought, "Good Lord. Here's a guy trying to lose my business and I'm not going to let him lose it." So he said, "What's the problem here." I told him I needed to exchange the gloves and so forth. He said, "You got a receipt?" I said, "Yeah, at home." He said, "Look, put yourself in my position." I thought, "That's an interesting approach." He said, "Could you, in good conscience, sell a pair of *used*," he sounded like he was spitting the word out, "*used* gloves as if they were new?" I said, "No, but these aren't *used* gloves, they just spent the night at my house. Now, put yourself in my position." He said, "Okay, how's that?" I said, "I bought my last motorcycle here." He said, "Yeah, that big Honda ST1100." I said, "That cost me at the time probably $12,000 with all the things that I got on it." He said, "Yeah." I said, "Before that I bought that Kawasaki for about $10,000. I spend about $2,500 a year on parts and service here. I also buy accessories to the tune of about $1,000 a year." He said, "Yeah, you're a great customer for us." I paused just to see if that was going to sink in. It didn't. "In light of the fact that I'm a really good customer for you and over the next few years I'm probably worth $40,000 in future business, does it make sense for you to lose all that future business over the dollar you're going to *gain* in a glove exchange?" There was this long pause and he looked at me—I wasn't sure how he was going to react but then finally he just said, "Would you like a bag for those or do you just want to wear them home?" I thought, "Alright! We finally got somewhere."

I realized afterwards when I was reflecting on that that what had happened was I had moved from one file in his mind to another. The file I started out in was the annoyance file. You know, here's a jerk coming in here trying to get an exception to our policy. When I pointed out to him what a great asset I was, I moved from the annoyance file to the asset file and he started realizing I was worth $40,000 to his business. You don't treat $40,000 the way you treat annoyances.

Wright

I'm glad it was you. I would have probably walked on the first guy.

Cathcart

Well, see, I'm in the business of doing relationship selling training and writing books on that so I consider each of these things to be sort of an experiment. One time I got in an argument with my wife over something and she said, "Didn't you know what I meant?" I said, "Yeah." She said, "Then why are you dragging this out?" I said, "Because I need this for a seminar." She started laughing and so did I. I said, "I'm sorry."

Wright

Jim, you're recognized as one of the world's greatest speakers. In fact, I had found, like we discussed in the intro, that there are only five speakers in the world who hold the same honors that you have attained. So, what "how-tos" do you give your training participants that are terrific and useful in regards to customer service?

Cathcart

The main thing that I cover is within the concept of relationship selling. I cover a concept I developed years ago called "Up-Serving." Some people say, "Oh, it's just a play on words like up-selling." I say, "No, it's a change in mentality." Up-selling means you bought X from me and I'm going to try and sell you X+1. So, I say, "You want fries with that?" or "Why don't you get two?" or "Oh, but wait! For only $19.95"...whatever. That's up-selling. But up-serving is different in that it has a different intent and a different function. For example, if I were up-selling, my goal would be to get you to buy more so I would put emphasis on whatever would cause you to purchase the next thing, right? Up-serving doesn't focus on getting you to buy more, it focuses on increasing not the transaction, but rather your satisfaction. So, if I say to myself going into the relationship with you in a business deal, "I want to up-serve. I want to make this deal, but then I want to look for ways to make him be even more satisfied at the end of this transaction than he might have been otherwise." So, I start getting creative and looking for little ways to add a personal touch, a little follow through or help guide you in the initial use of the product or service or I offer you a bonus that doesn't cost me much but provides you the ability to enjoy the product more. In up-serving what I get is a more satisfied customer and the bonus, happy news, is that I also usually get a bigger sale. The more satisfied someone is, the less resistant they are. The less resistant they are, the more open and trusting they will be and the more likely they are to say, "Could I get this extra feature as well? How much more would that be?" Then they don't quibble with you over price as much because they don't suspect that you're trying to take advantage of them.

Wright

Let me see if I've got this. It's a great concept. Rather than selling the "biggie fries," what you're doing is augmenting the experience?

Cathcart

Exactly. You can still sell the fries if you want. Now this is not a great application for that example because in a fast food business, you want the service to go rapidly without too much burden on the seller. But in a more complex selling environment, let's say that that person was indeed selling a hamburger, fries and a drink. You might say to the person, "Here's your burger cooked exactly the way you wanted it. By the way, we found that most of the people here absolutely love the french fries. They find that the fries make the enjoyment of the hamburger even better. Would you like to get some of our fries?" Doing it like that you are focused on enhancing their dining experience. They might say, "Well how much?" You say, "X dollars," and they say, "That's too much." Fine. Leave it alone. Give them a couple of fries for a sample. What's it going to cost you? Nothing. Just let them taste a couple of fries. You might say, like the Sommeliers in fine restaurants a lot of times come over—not the snooty types that try to make you think they're better than you because they know wine and you don't, but the ones that really want you to enjoy your dining experience— you say, "I'd like to get my wine by the glass instead of buying a bottle. Do you have some nice wine by the glass?" They say, "Yes, we've got a couple of very nice reds, a Merlot and a cabernet. Which would you prefer?" "I don't know." They say, "Let me give you a sample. Let me give you a little taste of the Merlot." That kind of thinking—it's not the act, I mean you certainly can't say, "I sell earth moving equipment. Here's a sample earth mover." But there are ways to take that thinking and apply it to selling a service, selling technology, selling whatever.

Wright

I've heard that great customer service begins with great selling skills. Is that your take?

Cathcart

Well, I'd say it begins with exceptional selling mentality because the mindset is everything in selling. It's not the technique, it's mindset. Let me prove that. When you go to buy something, if you encounter someone who you are convinced is genuinely trying to help, you will allow them to mess up in the way they're selling. You'll allow them to be awkward, you'll allow them to mumble, you'll allow them to be a little slow getting things done or be awkward in setting up a demonstration. You'll give them a lot of slack if you believe that they are genuinely trying to be of service to you. On the other hand, if you think or suspect that they are trying to persuade you to buy something whether you need it or not, you won't give them any slack at all. If they pause for a minute on the telephone, you'll hang up. They walk away from the counter for a moment to get a piece of information, you'll walk out of the dealership. So, the mentality is the main thing. Selling mentality is, "I am here to help people acquire what they will benefit from. I'm here to help people through the sell of my product of service."

Wright

That is customer service.

Cathcart

That's true. The selling process, of course, I guess the cardinal rule goes back to I used to use as our company slogan and that was "Selling is like medicine in that prescription before diagnosis is malpractice." So the number one skill in selling is to listen well and diagnose what the needs are before you start prescribing a solution to people.

Wright

One of your speech topics is the *Grandma Factor*, lifelong customer loyalty. You have written that everyone knows how to provide good service but your challenge is getting them to want to. What do you mean by that?

Cathcart

If you go back to what you asked earlier, "Should common decency and respect for people lead the way in customer service," absolutely. We all know how to be good people; respectful, appropriate, caring and that sort of thing. The key is to get people to behave that way on the job. A lot of companies try to get people to behave that way by giving them a hard-structured script of what they have to say. They think the words will convey the feelings, which is not necessarily so. I would rather spend time coaching someone in how to think about our customers, how to think about what our product or service does for people, how to think about understanding someone's needs so that the salesperson doesn't go in there thinking about themselves and what they're going to say. They go into a relationship thinking about the customer and what they need so they can respond a lot more genuinely.

When I talk about lifelong customer loyalty, a lot of companies think this is about getting the customer to be loyal to them. I think it should be the other way around. Lifelong customer loyalty means, if you're my customer I'm loyal to you, even when you don't buy from me. Take a common example, say automobiles. Everybody over a period of a lifetime will buy as many as, I don't know, a dozen automobiles maybe—used and new. If a person is going to buy a dozen automobiles, it's pretty certain they're not going to buy 12 of the same car.

Wright

Right.

Cathcart

And probably not 12 of the same brand. So, let's say I work for Honda and you come in and buy a car from me. I make a customer file and get as much information about you and your driving habits and your situation as I can so I can stay in touch and understand your needs. Let's say that I stay in touch with you, I'm loyal to you instead of you being loyal to me. I'm loyal to you now because you are my customer. I find a year from now that you've traded your Honda and gotten a Chevrolet. Well, a lot of businesses would say, "That's it. He's a traitor. He left me." No. All he did was trade cars. He's still there so stay loyal to him. You know, call him and ask, "How's your Chevy?" He'll say, "Fine, but I'm not going to buy a Honda." "I understand that. I just wanted to know how you're enjoying your Chevy and what you like about it...Really? Good. Well, it was nice talking to you." Then you come back in a few months with another contact, maybe a little article or gift or piece of information and at the same time you emphasize something about the next Honda that has a little more appeal than what he was saying he liked most about his new Chevy. Maybe next time he'll come buy a Honda.

So, people become loyal to brands because they feel a loyalty from the brand to them. That's not always the case, but it's often the case. You know, it's like people say, "I buy a Harley." Why do you buy a Harley? "Well, because it's American made." Why else? "Because it's a part of what this country is all about." They buy a Harley because of what Harley represents to them. It represents freedom. It represents individuality. It represents America. It represents all kinds of things. Despite the fact that Harley Davidsons often have Japanese carburetors in them. You know, they say it's American made. Sure it is, but some of those parts are bought overseas and brought to America, just like some of those foreign bikes and cars are built in America by companies outside of America. So, it's not always exactly what people say. The feelings behind that are what is driving it. If we can understand those feelings, we can understand those people.

Wright

You know, obviously selling skills demand self-motivation. You speak about the "Acorn Principle" as you help people grow in their profession. What is the Acorn Principle?

Cathcart

Well, I wrote a book a few years ago called *The Acorn Principle* to convey this simple message. Everyone of us has inside of us a seed of potential. The seed inside of you is different from the seed inside of me, although there may be a lot of overlaps and similarities. I think our greatest joy and greatest success in life comes from finding out what that seed is and then aligning our life so that seed gets the perfect opportunity to grow. What I mean by that is, let's say that I find I really enjoy working with numbers—which, by the way, is not the case but for some people it is—if I really enjoy working with numbers, then no matter where I'm at in my career and no matter what kind of business I'm involved in, I should make time to work with numbers because if I do I'm going to get better at it. You always get better more rapidly at what you're good at than what you are not good at. So, you develop your strengths, as Peter Drucker said, and you make your weaknesses irrelevant. In order to improve your weaknesses, you work to compensate for your weaknesses with something and then focus on your strengths so your advancement comes rapidly.

I believe that knowing yourself, which is what Socrates advised us to do, is a lifelong project. So I wrote the book *The Acorn Principle* with the subtitle *Know Yourself to Grow Yourself*. I made it just a self-guided tour of you. Understand how you're intelligent because there are different ways of being intelligent. Some people are people smart, some are number smart, some are musically smart, some are physically smart. There are all kinds of different smarts. Know your personal velocity. Know whether you're best at a real fast pace or a more leisurely pace. Learn to stay within the zone that's your natural zone. Learn your behavioral style so that you know how you come across to other people and how to use that. Know what background imprints have been left on you so that you know how to manage your background. You can't change your background, but you can add to it each day some new, positive experience that ultimately changes the overall effect of your background.

There are lots of things like that, like understanding the values that matter to you so you can see why you are you in favor of some things and against other things. The better you understand you, the more accepting you are of who you are so you spend less time being judgmental and self conscious. What happens is the better you know yourself, the better you can put the attention on the customer and listen to them and be a much more service-oriented professional.

Wright

Many years ago I took a three-day course on "Adventures in Attitude." The course was life changing. In the framework of that they gave me a DISC profile and I've been taking one about once a year since 1973. I mean, it's like taking an Aspirin a day. It kind of keeps me focused and thinking, "Am I still this and am I still that." But I'm personally surprised at the accuracy of those things.

Cathcart

That was developed by Dr. John Geier. Geier was the one who gave the Adventures in Attitudes people, who ultimately became Performax, sort of the backbone of their technology. Bob Conklin and Leo Houser were a couple of the people who were the leaders of the Adventures in Attitudes programs.

Wright

Yeah, Conklin was the one I knew.

Cathcart

Tony Alessandra and I went back years ago to the same works that John Geier was getting his research from—which was everybody from William Marsden to Carl Jung, all the way back to Hippocrates. We studied behavioral patterns and came up with a model that we call Relationship Strategies for Dealing with the Differences in People. Tony calls that today The Platinum Rule: Treat people the way they want to be treated. It measures the four things measured in DISC. For our listeners who aren't familiar with DISC, it measures four aspects of personality: Dominance, Interactiveness, Steadiness and Compliance. Tony and I found that there were four patterns people fall into as far as how they come across to other people in the world. That's the Director Pattern, highly forceful, dominant and direct; the Socializer Patter, which is interactive, playful and outspoken; the Relater Pattern, which is the steady, easygoing, relatable and amiable type; and the Thinker Pattern, which is the compliant, systematic, structured and reserved type. The better you understand those types and how each one of them behaves the better you understand how to deal with them and bring the tension level down, get the trust level up and get business.

Wright

I used to be a fairly angry and arrogant guy in my 20s and 30s. I was really successful in business and I think that contributed to it somewhat. Then, after really getting into personality profiling, I saw my anger subside and really I studied...

Cathcart

Pardon me for interrupting, but do you think that's a result of understanding yourself better and being less judgmental of yourself?

Wright

Either that...well, I did kind of take it easier on myself, but more than that I think I took it easier on everybody. I just found out that the study of you is the study of me. You know, we're a whole lot alike, you and I. If you've ever loved someone then so have I and I can kind of understand that. We've had almost the same kinds of feelings at one time or another. So I started looking at people differently and now I cut people more slack than I ever have.

Cathcart

Well said.

Wright

I think that profiling did it. I know you're an expert in relationship selling. Could you give us your definition of relationship selling?

Cathcart

Sure. Back in the early '80s, the term wasn't being widely used. I was teaching that concept and I didn't really know how to say it in one simple phrase until one day it hit me...Relationship Selling. Relationship being a soft word and selling being perceived as a hard word. Put those two together and it made an interesting new impression. So I wrote a book on that and I started teaching under that phrase. Everybody picked up on it. At first people resisted. They said, "You need to choose. It's either a relationship or a sale." Back in the hard selling days I guess that was true. But today if you don't cultivate a relationship—a sense of trust and connection with people—they don't want to buy from you and they won't because there are too many good options. You used to have to worry about whether something was good or bad. Today, almost all the choices available to you are pretty good choices. Relationship selling is a form of doing business that puts the emphasis on establishing and sustaining a trusting connection with your customer.

Wright

Is that hard to do?

Cathcart

No, it's not. Not if your intention is to connect and be trustworthy in that connection.

Wright

I've had several psychologists down through the years tell me that everyone loves to buy because it's a drive. But those same people also hate to be sold. It sounds kind of strange. You know, you love to buy but you hate to be sold. How can that be?

Cathcart

Well, the difference is who is in control. You love to buy because buying is an acquisition and acquisition is an expansion of your life. That's just a life-impulse seeking expression. Seeking more growth, more opportunity and more possibilities. So, people love to acquire things and try new things. People tell you, "Oh, people are resistant to change." No. People are resistant to change in their comfortable routines, but they *love* change when it comes to a new stereo, a new car, and new TV., a new outfit to wear or place to go out to eat. People love change. People absolutely adore buying. What they don't like is imposed change. What they don't like is being forced or manipulated into buying. What they don't like is buying something when they haven't yet determined whether they can trust the person who is selling. So that's the whole point. Where does the control come from, you or the other person? If I trust you, then I don't care where it comes from. If you recommend it, I say, "Well, he recommended it. It might be good for me I might as well go along and say yes." If I don't trust you, I say, "Wait a minute, who do you think you are? I'm in control of me."

Wright

Your relationship selling book was leading edge and considered revolutionary, in fact, in the mid-'80s. But your latest book *The Eight Competencies of Relationship Selling* is setting a new standard. Could you tell our readers a little bit about it?

Cathcart

You bet! When I wrote the first book, I was fortunate to be the first person to write a book under that title. So, it caught on and is still selling today in countries all around the world. *Relationship Selling* is in Chinese, Japanese, Finnish, German and I don't know how many other languages and it's taught at colleges and universities. It's doing well. But the concept is now widely accepted so it's gotten to the point where people say, "Relationship selling, that's what we do." They just take it for granted. So when I went to rewrite the book I started back with my original research then I took all the customer experience of about 17 years of teaching the other concept and using it with different clients and wrote the new book focusing on eight areas of sales ability, which I called "competencies." Each of those "competencies" is a set of different skills that makes you good at one aspect of selling versus another.

For example, the eight competencies are: Preparation, which includes sales- and self-preparation—you can be good at one and not good at the other or you can be good at both; Targeting, both the right people and the right sales approach with those people; Connecting with the persons head, their intellect, and the person's heart, their emotions, so that they feel good about doing business with you; Assessing the needs of the situation based on the circumstances and also the needs of the person and how they feel about the situation and the gap between those two things. Also assess the needs of the person. Here's what you have now. Here is how you feel about it. Here's what you could do next. So you assess both the situation and the person. Then you solve the problem. So solving is the next—which would be typically referred to as the presentation aspect of selling. But in relationship selling there is much more dialogue so it's not just one person presenting it's two people talking. In solving the problem there are two parts: solving the main problem, let's say you need a computer. I can get you a computer and that solves your main problem. But that's just solving your need. I might also recognize that I need to solve your want. So maybe what you want is a computer with a flat screen instead of a larger monitor. Maybe what you want is a laptop computer instead of a desktop computer. Maybe you want to use a palm pilot or something like that. So in solving I want to make sure I solve your main problem but at the same time that I solve your "felt problem;" needs and wants. Next, commitment. That's a big part of selling. If you don't get commitment, there wasn't any selling there was just discussion. So, I need two things. I need to be good at getting you to agree to a solution and commit to that. You know, "Yes, Jim, this is a good computer and this is what I should get. I absolutely agree with you. Yup, the price is good. Sounds good to me." "Alright, David, let's go ahead and buy today." "Well, I'll get back to you." Okay, I got commitment to the solution, but I didn't get commitment to the action. So the other side of commitment, which would be closing in most people's form of selling, is getting people to commit to the action and take action today. A lot of people criticize the lack of using the word "closing." They say, "Wait a minute. Everybody knows what closing is." Yes, but the problem with closing as a concept is that it came out of the industrial era mentality. The type of selling thought that says, "I'm here to persuade you to buy." Now if I go in with a relationship selling attitude, my belief is that I'm here to help you make the right decision and take action on it now or in the most appropriate way. So I'm not just here to persuade you to buy, I'm here to help you make a good decision. If my product is not right for you, I'm not going to sell you my product because that would be exploiting you and losing a customer anyway sooner or later.

So, closing is a deal mentality. That's when you shut something and it's finalized. What I want to do is confirm the sale. So if you want to buy something or need to buy something I want you to commit to the solution I've offered and commit to taking action on that. I want to confirm that you bought, not close anything. I want to open up the dialogue and the relationship. Hence, the elimination of the word "closing." So we go from the commitment phase to the next to the last which is: Assuring. The assuring competency deals with two parts. Assuring that the customer is satisfied—and that takes certain types of skills—and then assuring that the customer remains satisfied and loyal—and that requires a different set of skills. So then the final phase is the management competency. That's when you're managing sales and you are managing yourself as a sales professional. So there are the eight. You've got Preparation, Targeting, Connecting, Assessing, Solving, Committing, Assuring Satisfaction and Managing Yourself and Your Sales.

Wright

That's very interesting. Does the Assuring competency create a situation where buyer's remorse is less and less?

Cathcart

Exactly, because buyers remorse happens when someone has made a buying decision and forgot specifically why they made it. Where it was all an emotional decision with no logic behind it or no supporting documentation or proof that it was a good choice and shame on the seller because the seller didn't do a good job of educating or equipping the buyer to justify and reinforce their decision after it was over. For example, a person goes out to buy something and let's say they go into a store and buy an appliance and they get it home and announce to their spouse that they bought an appliance and the spouse says, "Why did you buy that? It seems like too much money for that type of an appliance." Well, they think, "Gosh, I wish I had the salesperson here. It made so much sense at the time." Well, if I were the salesperson, I would say, first off, "Thank you for buying this appliance. Here's a brochure that tells you specifically how this works for you and why this is such a special value. Second, here are four key items that I think make this a really solid decision. Let me note these for you because these are the main reasons that it makes good sense for you to say yes to this today. By the way, delivery will happen on Tuesday. John will be the guy driving the truck. He'll come in and help you get it set up." So I give you an orientation as to what is coming next. Now I've done a couple of things. One, I've reassured you it was a good decision. Two, I've given you information and tools so that you can explain to other people why it's a good decision. Three, I've told you what's coming next so that there is no long gap of wondering what's going to happen before you hear from our people or see your product. So buyer's remorse goes away. There's no need for it.

Wright

You know, I have read that you believe that business should be practiced primarily as an act of friendship rather than a process of negotiation. Is it possible to establish friendship in a brief sales experience?

Cathcart

I think you absolutely can. Now, obviously deep friendship requires time and multiple exposures to one another. But friendship is a basic human dynamic. If I see you on the street and we've never met before and make eye contact in a friendly non-threatening way, there is a connection. So at some level, friendship is a dynamic that is always present—or it may be lacking because of some perceived animosity. If someone thinks you are a threat, the friendship doesn't develop. But if they see that they can trust you, the friendship has room to grow. So how do you cultivate that? Keep adding to the trust level.

For example, friendly eye contact or common courtesy, as you were talking about earlier, just basic human decency and respect for the other person. If you get involved in a conversation and you take interest in them instead of only talking about yourself and your company then the friendship grows even further. If you do what you say you will do on time and in a professional manner, and you don't try to make excuses for your own shortcomings, you just make things right, then the friendship continues to grow.

So I think business should be approached from this point of view. If you and I decide to go into business together and we say, "Let's get out there and build some profitable friendships." So we start looking for who it would be profitable for us to have friendships with and we identify our targeted market. Then we say, "Those kinds of people, what do they consider to be friendly behavior? What sort of friendly acts could we perform, in a business context, that would cause those people to want to stay connected with us so we can get all of their business over time instead of just today's business?" Then we approach everything, even problem solving and policy making. When you set policies in your company, if you set the policies to protect you from the evil customers that might take advantage, you're going to end up losing all kinds of customers because you're just not friendly to deal with. If you set your policies to bond you with the potential customers that you want, then maybe you'll waste a little from time to time and be taken advantage of slightly on occasion, but most of all you'll be winning new customers that wouldn't have come to you otherwise. Look at the businesses you know of where they do that versus those where they don't and you can tell very rapidly which one is trying to assume honesty on the part of the customer and which one is trying to assume dishonesty on the part of the customer. Which one do you want to go to next? Given the option, you'll always go to the one who assumes you are honest. You say, "Yeah, but what about the people who rip you off?" It is the cost of doing business. If your policies are so lose that anyone can rip you off, then shame on you. That was a very unintelligent way to set policy. But your policies should be liberal enough to allow people to do something creative, something thoughtful, something nice and not have to make it fit a rigid form every single time.

Wright

Well, what an interesting conversation. I really appreciate it. You know, I've been booking speakers for 13 years and I've found that, very much like you, a lot of my friends are speakers, and I've found that when they train they're training the whole body, mind and spirit. Getting people to understand that selling—whether it's preparation, targeting, connecting, assessing, solving, commitment, assuring or managing—no matter what they're doing they're still human beings and that it is important to treat people that way. You certainly have been forthcoming and very helpful in this conversation, Jim, and I really appreciate it.

Cathcart

Well, thank you. It has been a joy for me and I thoroughly enjoyed this conversation. I look forward to the next one.

About The Author

Among professional speakers worldwide, Jim Cathcart is an industry leader. He has risen to the top of his profession through more than 25 years of presentations to a worldwide audience and decades of unselfish service to his profession. He believes in serving his industry as well as his customers.

Jim Cathcart

Cathcart Institute, Inc.

Speakers Office

6120 Paseo Del Norte, Ste. M-2

Carlsbad, California 92009

Phone: 800.222.4883

Phone: 760.603.8110

Fax: 760.603.8010

Email: Info@Cathcart.com

www.Cathcart.com

Chapter 10

ANNE M. OBARSKI

THE INTERVIEW

David E. Wright (Wright)
Today we are talking to Anne M. Obarski. She is the Customer Service Spy, an internationally published author, professional speaker, and retail consultant. Anne is also founder and Executive Director of Merchandise Concepts, a Pittsburgh, Pennsylvania, based consulting service since 1984. Anne works with companies who want to create service strategies to keep their customers coming back. Her retail snoops have mystery shopped well over 2,000 stores and businesses looking for excellence in customer service. Guess what? She's still looking. She is past president of the National Speakers Association, Pittsburgh Chapter, of which she received the Chapter Member of the Year 2000 award. Anne is the author of the books *Applied Retail Mathematics, Surprising Secrets of Mystery Shoppers,* as well as a contributing author to *Real World Customer Service Strategies That Really Work.* Her newest edition is a customer service and sales training program titled *What Customers Wish You Knew.* Anne, welcome to our conversation today, and thank you for being with us.

Anne M. Obarski (Obarski)
Thank you for having me.

Wright

You call yourself the Customer Service Spy. How did that start?

Obarski

That title recently came from one of my clients. I think he was teasing, but it actually stuck! I must admit that it does get a reaction out of people. It's almost like saying I'm a food expert. Immediately, people imagine me coming into their businesses, just as if it were a restaurant, trying to find something that doesn't leave a good taste in my mouth!

I am not looking necessarily for a "bad taste," but I feel I have become the service strategist that can help businesses make little changes in how they do business that can have a big effect on their customers.

Wright

You know I've heard about mystery shopping all my life, but I've never talked to anyone who has actually done it. Could you tell our readers a little bit more about mystery shopping?

Obarski

I'm glad you asked that question. In my corporate background, which goes back well over 25 years, we used to have mystery shoppers who would come into our stores at various times.

I remember being shopped myself many years ago where the mystery shopper filled out a little postcard that had very few questions on it, mostly dealing with how the customer was greeted. Since that time, mystery shopping has grown drastically. I believe that companies are interested in finding out much more about what the customer thinks and feels and if they are smart, willing to do whatever it takes to make the improvements that the *customer* thinks are important.

My business began working solely as a retail consultant back in 1984. At that time, my work as a consultant was focused on inventory management and financial planning. As my business grew I realized that many companies, large and small, had a handle on the "business" side of their business. They understood buying and merchandising and even marketing, but far too often did not see their businesses through their customer's eyes and in turn, what *made* them loyal customers. I believe it was about what I call the "soft skills" or the true customer service skills that just might be missing.

I was asked to do a mystery shop for a local mall and I just used my college instructor background to make up the questions that would give the client the best information they could use to improve their businesses, which would eventually come right from the mouth's of their own customers.

Since about 1990, I have been offering my clients a complete mystery shopping program. We customize evaluation forms. We hire people. We train them. We assign the shoppers. We calculate the forms, and then we deliver the feedback to the client.

But let me say that mystery shopping only works well when it is used as a *system*. Once we have done an initial mystery shop we can pin point the areas within the business that are great and those that need some help.

Our forte is to offer to develop a customized training program to focus on the areas where there's a need for improvement. Once the employees have been trained we urge our clients to build in an "accountability factor" into their employees reviews. This is a great way to urge employees to be committed to their performance at work.

And we return to do the evaluations as often as the client wishes, which we suggest are done at least once a month and that way we provide on-going feedback. It's all about developing and delivering the level of customer service that you really want to be known for.

Wright

So what makes a good mystery shopper?

Obarski

You know, every time I mention that mystery shopping is part of my business, I get people begging to work for me as one of my mystery shoppers. I think it is a silent wish of so many people that they would love to have the opportunity to really tell some companies how they think they could improve their businesses. If you think I'm crazy, just start a conversation about service the next time you are out to dinner with friends and you'll see what I mean!

But just venting isn't the real basis for what makes a good mystery shopper.

You know, I almost look at it like choosing a jury member. If you've ever been chosen for jury duty, you know they go through an awful lot of questions and there are certain people that they are looking for.

And maybe that really is my focus. I look for someone who's already had some type of a background working in a service business. When you're working with the public, which could be anything from working for a dry cleaner, or in a restaurant, or a hair salon, or a corporate retail establishment, to gosh, it could be anything that is considered part of the service industry, you already come to the table with expectations of customer service...

We also look for people who are articulate and who write well. People who are fair and non-ego driven.

I've had some horror stories in my life as a mystery shopping company where we've had some people who thought it would be very interesting to see if they could get a reaction out of the people they were shopping by actually telling them that they were mystery shopping them and they were there to get them! So I've looked at trying to not have an ego come into play.

And I also look for people who can "think on their feet" and come up with questions they can ask an employee to test their knowledge about the company they work for, the products they offer or specifics about their services.

The special trait I try to look for is that of efficiency. I need people who are efficient in getting their information back on time and completed very professionally. I don't want to be put in the position of having to rewrite wording or descriptions of situations so that they sound tactful and professional.

Wright

Do most companies use mystery shopper service? And if not, why?

Obarski

Well, I believe that the number continues to rise in popularity. The question really is whether or not they are really willing to make the *commitment* of using a mystery shopping service which means taking a serious look at their "warts" and make the decision to do something about them before they become cancerous.

Many companies believe that their business is just fine, that they don't need a program like this. But, I say that about 75% of businesses have tried it at least once. I know for a fact that some companies have made up their own little programs, brought in their sister Kathy or their mom to check out their service.

If they haven't used a service it might be because they don't know *who* to call or the companies themselves are ego driven and believe that they can do without it.

Wright
You know I can see a situation where a mystery shopper might go in and just get a sales person on a bad day. Does a client have the option of having two or three or perhaps four mystery shoppers shopping their location at the same time to get a better feel of how they work, or better yet, how their associates work and under pressure? Do you ever do that?

Obarski
We do recommend that we send in shoppers at different times into an establishment for exactly that reason.

And I will say, though, we remind our companies that a true "mystery shop," is what I call a *snapshot* in time.

What that means is, if I was a mystery shopper posing as a customer and I walk in to a place of business and the sales associate looks at me and tells me she has a migraine headache and they have told me in no uncertain terms that they feel lousy, I need to report it just that way. If she takes some medication and another shopper comes in an hour later, the whole scenario could very well be different. It truly is a *snapshot* in time.

The point that the client needs to understand is that both of these situations can represent a sampling of how typical customers are handled daily. Unfortunately, when an employee feels bad they might not be able to go home, they might not get a break and the customer starts looking more and more like an interruption to their day.

Employees need to be aware that the next customer they come in contact with may be coming in from out of town, it may be their first time into their store, and so now, as a customer, they are developing what I call *report card* based on the service they receive.

We realize that sometimes the customer is just going to catch the associate at the wrong time and that is exactly why we suggest doing a number of shops and not just basing the service they provide on the results of one shop. That isn't fair and that is not how we work.

We like to see what happens on a Monday morning or Thursday afternoon or how about a Friday evening or maybe a Saturday night just about ten minutes before a business closes. What kind of a service am I going to get then?

And then we like to go back to our clients and say, "These are our overall findings and we would like to talk about a couple of things that seem to continue to pop up that could be handled in a little more professional manner."

Wright
What is the biggest consistent problem your shoppers report?

Obarski
You probably could guess what it is. But I believe the number one problem that we hear over and over again is when shoppers will report, "I was made to feel invisible. No one noticed me. No one noticed I was there. I felt like I was wasting their time."

You know my favorite movie is the recent hit *Chicago*. There's a wonderful song in it called *Mr. Cellophane* with the lyrics that go something like, "You can see right through me, you never even knew I was there."

The number two complaint is that many sales associates and many frontline managers talk like robots or better yet, parrots, to their customers.

In other words, "thanks and have a nice day" comes out like it was programmed into them! I know that if I'm in line, I can bet my bottom dollar you're going to say the same thing to me as you just did to the customer in front of me. I'm just another transaction in your day. I'm just another cash cow, and I really don't make a difference.

So I think those two communication skills, what we call *soft skills*, could easily be fixed, if a company made a conscious decision to do so. It is so simple; open your eyes greet your customers like you would a guest in your home and treat them that way everyday no matter how you feel!

Wright
I remember walking into a retail establishment only yesterday, as a matter of fact it was a restaurant chain called, Cracker Barrel, and as I went in the door, someone said, "Welcome to the Cracker Barrel. We're glad you came in today." Or something like that, and I immediately looked around. I couldn't even tell who it was. And everyone I passed until I got to the lady who seats everyone, I have to say there must have been five people that welcomed me there. The reason I make that point is our culture is going to self service, and you know it brings back memories of how it used to be when I was a young driver,

you drove up to the service station, the guy opened your hood and did all kinds of things. Now you do it all yourself. You don't get that kind of service at the gas stations anymore and I can't find anybody in Wal-Mart to help me, you know, or a lot of places that I go. If you go up and down the aisles trying to find someone to ask where things are the likelihood of finding someone is slim, because it's all self service. Do you think that that has had an impact? In other words are the smaller numbers of sales associates who are working on the floor trying to give you some space to look, or are they too busy or just afraid to approach you? How would you solve that problem? The cellophane problem.

Obarski

The cellophane. I think there is a fine line when it comes to "self service" and whether sales associates feel it is their "job" to ask if you need assistance.

If you ask most people, "Do you like to be greeted when you walk into a store (i.e. the Wal-Mart greeter who asks you if you want a cart, and by the way, they also ask 50 people in front of you and 50 people behind you) or would you prefer to at least have someone within, as I say shouting distance, so that if I need help you are there to help me?"

I think most people would say it is almost a combination of the two, "Don't hound me, but I don't want to have to look very far if I have a question to ask or I need help."

Our whole society has become extremely efficient. Give me what I want, when I want it, as fast as you can. If you ask a kid whether they remember when someone pumped your gas, quite frankly, Dave, I doubt if they would remember that. But ask them where they want to go eat, and my guess it will be a "fast food" restaurant. It just boils down to what they have experienced when it comes to service and what their expectations are.

Wright

Right.

Obarski

I think we are so used to living in a self-serve society that when we encounter being greeted as you did at Cracker Barrel it's almost like you are taken back a little bit.

I think that in the service industries, and specifically in the retail industry, businesses have realized that they can cut a lot of their expenses by cutting their training and cutting the amount of full time sales associates from their budgets.

I believe it is a matter of manipulating their profit and loss margin, and there are only so many areas to cut. You can only buy so many things out of this country. You can only mark it up so high. You can only have so many associates on your floor. So one of the ways businesses try to improve their profit margin is to have less people on the selling floor.

And some of the savvy retailers are teaching you and me how to ring up our own merchandise. Grocery stores and Wal-Mart are getting proficient at it and I am seeing it even in Home Depot stores! You can check out your own lumber, paint, screw drivers and whatever else you have in your buggy.

Dave, I still believe that we are all multi-tasking at such high levels that there are certain times, when time is of the essence, when we need to have someone there to answer our questions.

Wright

You know I've read more books, listened to more tapes, gone to more seminars during the last 20 years on customer service than any other single topic. Yet customer service seems to me to be at an all time low. Why don't most customer service programs work?

Obarski

Well, I believe it all comes down to the desire to maintain *consistency and commitment* in serving the customer as a major part of a business.

When turnover in some stores runs over 80%, companies have a very hard time with those two words, *consistency and commitment.*

David, you know many companies who have had to cut their staffing in order to stay in business. Unfortunately, some have also decided to get rid of their training departments totally and bring in outside services to train their employees only once or twice a year. And we've all seen the statistics that show how it costs 2 1/2 times a persons salary to hire and train a new person to replace a lost one. Training costs are huge. If there is no *consistency* in training people as well as holding them *accountable* for what they are expected to do, that is where you and I keep encountering employees who can't answer the most basic of customer's questions. You can learn a skill, but if no one holds you accountable for it and you don't have any reason to use that skill, most of us will stop doing it. The customer has to then contend with a poorly trained, unmotivated employee and they turn on their heels and head out the door along with their business.

Some companies are even depending on seasoned employees to mentor new employees rather than providing on-going training programs. My question is, "How is the *consistency* in that kind of training monitored?"

Don't get me wrong Dave, there are companies out there who do absolutely wonderful jobs of training their associates, but it takes those two words to make it work well, *consistency and commitment.*

Sometimes I think businesses have so much to contend with that they bring in a mystery shopping company as almost a Band-Aid when they don't know what else to do after hearing that their service is less than desirable. It is a quick way to see if their training or lack of training is working. Too often, the mystery shopping feedback becomes the "stick" instead of the "carrot" and employees rebel when they are told they did not perform when they were mystery shopped. If training was *consistent* and employees were held *accountable* throughout the year, not just at review time, mystery shopping could be looked at more positively and have rewards linked to it.

Too often there is what I call "internal bleeding" where a company says, "We'll see what we're doing wrong. We'll see if we can heal the problem without spending much money or time." That is where the inconsistency comes into play, not only with external customer service, but internal customer service. There isn't a team effort from the top down and the loyalty of employees as well as customers is lost. That is why you will continue to see more books and programs and seminars on customer service because it seems like it is a hard lesson for companies to learn. It is not always about price, much of business is the business of building relationships.

Wright

So what do you think could be done differently to see successful results?

Obarski

Well, as I just said, I believe it starts at the top—top management believing and living the importance of service, and you know what, Dave, actually mirroring that throughout the organization.

It's the internal customer service that drives the external customer service. If I see my boss taking care of a customer and bending over backwards, getting their hands dirty, and actually waiting on a customer, I think that I might learn a little bit more from just seeing that.

I'd like to share an example. I was just reading on Inc.com about the President of Jet Blue, and how the President of Jet Blue has been seen on Jet Blue Airlines in an apron that says, "I'm the Chairman of the Board, and I'm here to serve you."

He mentioned how he would fly in his own planes and interview the passengers about the service and the flight all while walking up and down the aisle pouring coffee and "serving" his customers! He was really interviewing his customers trying very hard to find out what the company does well and what it could do better.

I could just imagine what was going through the minds of Jet Blue employees on the flight as he's pouring coffee, picking up the trash and asking "his customers" if they'd like a bag of peanuts.

It was an easy lesson showing the other employees that are on that flight that the owner of the company is willing to do whatever it takes to stay a step ahead of his competition before he gets blindsided by something that they're doing and he's learned what he should be doing, first hand, through his customers.

So I think that results will be achieved when top management believes in the importance of service, they are willing to invest in what it takes to deliver that service, to train, to hold employees accountable, to understand how to effectively give results from a performance audit, and last of all rewarding those employees in a way that will motivate them.

Just saying, "Well, we'll give you a pin with a few rhinestones in it" doesn't cut it with employees anymore. The key to any good reward system is for all levels of management to understand what motivates the individual people who work for them and to make a *commitment* and be *consistent* with that reward system.

Wright

What kind of reward system have you seen that works?

Obarski

The power in a reward system is how it is viewed by the employees. Frequently an employee will say, "Well, you know, we had a reward system, and I think I got $10.00 once in my paycheck. And, well, the company doesn't do that anymore."

They remember the one time, but when it stops, they wonder, "Was it me? Was it that the company didn't think it was important? Why did it stop?"

But interestingly, what motivates one person may not motivate another. Companies can invest in valuable assessment tools that can pinpoint an employee's behavioral style. They can further discover the key ways to communicate with that person as well as to obtain critical information on what motivates them as well.

The assessment tools are powerful, but they are only part of the picture. Building a relationship with your employees is probably the biggest piece of the puzzle. How much do you really know about the personal life of your employees? I'm not talking about soap opera material, but let's say that one of your employees has a couple of kids who are soccer players. Maybe a reward for that particular employee could be two tickets to a soccer game in town.

Or maybe that you know that your employee absolutely loves chocolate covered pretzels. So if they do a fabulous job on delivering customer service and you see it, or they do very well on a mystery shop program, you could bring them in a beautifully packaged box of chocolate covered pretzels.

Or maybe it's another employee that you know that just absolutely loves driving a beautifully washed and waxed car, and maybe there's a way that you can reward them with two or three car washes for the next three months.

The reward can personalize the relationship you have with your employee; this process can spill over into the customer/sales associate relationship as well. It might not be a material reward, but an "I remember something about you" verbal reward.

Example, Joe your best employee, thinks to himself, "Hum, I love talking to Mrs. Jones when she comes into the store. I know Mrs. Jones has a son that plays soccer, and I am going to remember to ask her about her son's soccer game. I know how good I feel when Mr. Smith, who's my boss, asks about my son's soccer game."

So now we have a relationship that is built on personal things that I know about my boss, my boss knows about me, and I know about my customer. So it's a relationship business and it's a relationship business built on communication skills.

Wright

I've had fun guessing at the answer to the next question that I'm going to ask you. And I'm really interested in your answer. Do you ever refuse to do a mystery shop?

Obarski

Well, I know it's not my interview, but I'd love to turn the tables in this interview and say, "Well, Dave, what was the one thing that you thought I would say?"

But I'll share mine and maybe then you'd like to share yours and we'll see if there is a match!

Yes, I have refused to do mystery shops and it seems as though that number is increasing!

Early on in my career I was actually asked to do a mystery shop in which I had to evaluate a specific manager, at a specific location and time of day. I didn't think much about it and I personally did the "shop."

Later, I found out he was fired the very next day. Worse yet, it was based on the feedback that I gave. It wasn't rude feedback. It was very professionally written and documented feedback, but none the less, that person was fired the very next day.

Worst of all, my client actually said, "Well, thank you very much for writing that information. I really just wanted to use your report as the *"last straw."*

I can't tell you how bad I felt and worse yet, I was made the scapegoat.

From that day on, I vowed I would never take on a mystery shopping job in which the company did not want to integrate the program into their customer service "system," but merely look at it as what I call a "motivational stick." Just a bullet point on their customer service agenda to be checked off when completed.

So when people say to me, "Well, I really don't want training, I just want you to come in and do a mystery shop." Or "I really don't want to do anything with this mystery shop, I just want to get my people on their toes," I usually advise them to find another company as I don't feel the "fit."

When the process is used as scare tactic, we have had employees say, "Oh we knew who the mystery shopper was. They were in today." And in actuality, that mystery shopper was never in the store, but the employees were so petrified they were second guessing each customer that walked through the door.

I never want to work for a company who wants to create such a fear factor in their employees so that I come across as the bad guy that could provide the information that would jeopardize their job.

Most recently I've refused to do a mystery shop, when in my heart-of-hearts as a consultant; I felt that the results of a mystery shop may not necessarily provide them with the information to what the underlying problem was.

Frequently companies say, "Oh, business isn't good, I think there is something wrong with our customer service so I need a mystery shop done."

I really need to know more about what is going on in the whole company, because we may just end up trying to treat the symptoms, but not treating what is actually the underlying factor. It really is like being a private eye!! Maybe that "Customer Service Spy" title is a fit, Dave!

I start looking for clues. I begin by talking to people in management as well as the frontline employees. I start focus groups and ask as many questions as I can to get the critical feedback.

And sometimes, a slump in business can be tracked back to a personality conflict between managers. It can be something that was said a long time ago, and someone is carrying a grudge. It can be something that is so deep-seated, as I say, a cancer, and if that cancer is not corrected and treated, it will continue to grow until it eats up the entire organization.

That is where some companies turn to a mystery shop to be the Band-Aid for a far more serious problem.

So I don't know if those two answers were what you had in your mind, David, but I think you probably understand why I stand my ground!

Wright

Well actually, the first reason was exactly what I was thinking. In fact I was thinking of it in legal terms. If the owner of the company used you to terminate someone, and used that as part of documentation, boy I'd love to be the lawyer on the other side!

Obarski

Isn't that the truth!

Wright

I think what you're uncovering is that if company owners are really serious about hiring your services as a mystery shopper, what they are trying to do is pin-point the things that they can improve on and be better at. And so it might result in training to do that. I can see where that would be a tremendous service. Through your eyes, what will it take for companies to gain the respect and loyalty of their customers in the future?

Obarski

I think in the past few years we've seen a roller coaster ride in how all of us do business with companies that we see on a day- to-day basis.

Whether it's our dentist, our doctor, the company that we choose to fly with when we travel, the hotels, the dry cleaners, wherever we trade our money for goods or services, I think each and every one of us wants to do business with people we *trust.*

And I think that level of trust, as I have said throughout this interview, starts the building process from the top management right down to the frontline employees. That trust is built through relationships with knowledgeable employees. Those companies whose policy is making sure that an employee is never ever put on the phone or in front of a client or a perspective customer without having been completely trained in the services the company offers, the products they have, what the products do, when the customer can get them, how they're delivered, and everything that goes with showing the customer that they are a professional sounding employee.

Secondly, living in such a busy world, I believe people want to do business with people who are *efficient.* How quickly can things get done? Can I count on you? Everybody's life is hectic. So the efficiency factor is key.

The example you gave earlier in the interview about a full service gas station was not far off the mark. If pumping my own gas is just part of today's environment, then when I come up to the gas pumps on a busy morning, one of the things I absolutely hate to see are the little trash bags over the handle of the pump that tells me I can't get gas at this station.

That is a visual sign that screams, "Want gas? Go elsewhere!"

Companies are also sending customers away by having an inefficient way of handling problems through their phone systems. When I call my internet provider and I want to find out why my internet isn't working. I don't want to have to have to choose one of seven options in the first menu, and then go to another menu, just to hear that what I want isn't in that list either. I have to admit I may have "lied" in the past when that little prompt says, "If you have a rotary phone please remain on the line for the next available agent." Yes, a live person! Here's my question, what 30-something even knows what a rotary phone is?

Bottom line, I believe people want to do business with people who are *efficient* and make it easy to do business with them.

Wright

Right.

Obarski

And lastly, I believe that people want to do business with people who are *friendly*. I am not saying they need to be your best friend, but those employees that can answer questions effectively and efficiently with good verbal skills and good eye contact get my business. Through those strong communication skills, they can develop that relationship that creates what I call the "boomerang customer." If I am a business owner, I want customers who I have a trusting relationship with, continue to come back to buy from me and hopefully, in the process, tell others to do so as well.

David, it really still comes back to the emphasis that the company puts on training their employees to daily mirror the principles that the company was founded on. So when companies continue to reduce their training and staffing budgets, I think customers feel a disconnect between their advertising and what they truly stand for, and then loyalty and trust goes out the door. I think it's important for companies not to look at their customers like a dollar sign with feet because they can and they will go somewhere else, and it's probably going to be to their competition.

Wright

Well, how interesting. I've really enjoyed this, and I certainly appreciate you taking this time out this morning to talk to me about this really intelligent and needed service.

Obarski

Well, thank you very much. I hope that the readers will gain that insight as well out of this time that we've spent together.

Wright

Today we've been talking to Anne M. Obarski. She is the Customer Service Spy. Her snoops have mystery shopped well over 2,000 stores and businesses. And the part I like about that is they're still looking for excellence in customer service, and you'd better watch out. She may come into your store one day. Thank you so much, Anne, for being with us today on *Conversations on Customer Service and Sales*.

Obarski

Oh, it has truly been my pleasure, Dave.

About The Author

Anne M. Obarski is the "Eye" on Performance. She is an author, professional speaker and retail consultant. For almost two decades, Anne has been the Executive Director or Merchandise Concepts, a Pittsburgh, PA based retail-consulting service. Anne works with companies who are people, performance, and profit focused and helps leaders see their businesses through their customer's eyes.

She is known for her educational and motivational approach to handling business owners' two major problems: selling merchandise or services profitably and maintaining repeat and referral customers. Her company's mystery shoppers, better known as "Retail Snoops," have secretly "snooped" over 2000 stores searching for excellence in customer service.

Her topics include customer service, sales, communication skills, and image. She is Past President of the National Speakers Association—Pittsburgh, PA Chapter, and active in the National Speakers Association since 1996, and sits on the board of a number of non-profit associations.

Anne M. Obarski

Merchandise Concepts

121 Kathy Ann Ct.

McMurray, Pennsylvania 15317

Phone: 724.941.4149

Fax: 724.941.4304

Email: anne@merchandiseconcepts.com

www.merchandiseconcepts.com

Chapter 11

DAN KOSCH

MARK SHONKA

THE INTERVIEW

David E. Wright (Wright)

Today we are talking to Dan Kosch and Mark Shonka. They are co-authors of *Beyond Selling Value*, as well as, numerous articles in national and trade publications, and IMPAX Corporation Co-Presidents. Together, they have tallied more than 45 years of experience in direct sales, sales leadership, sales consulting, and training. IMPAX, a leading sales performance improvement company, is committed to helping clients improve their sales, account management, and sales leadership efforts to drive business results. IMPAX has worked with thousands of sales professionals in the field and the classroom throughout North America and abroad. Shonka and Kosch are highly sought after authorities on a range of sales topics including selling value, strategic account selling, strategic account management and sales leadership. With names like IBM, 3M, Dupont, Eli Lilly, D&B, US Bank and Microsoft, the authors' client list represents some of the world's leading sales organizations. Mark and Dan, welcome to *Conversations on Customer Service and Sales*!

Dan Kosch (Kosch)
Thank you, David.

Mark Shonka (Shonka)
We're glad to be here.

Wright
Mark, let me ask you the first question. What are the trends you're seeing related to selling and selling value in particular?

Shonka
There are some fascinating trends right now that are affecting direct sales. For instance, challenging economic conditions are affecting everyone domestically and internationally, often restricting and delaying decisions. For this and other reasons, competition is very aggressive and sometimes even desperate. As many of us have seen, this competition is also increasingly global in nature.

Another trend we see is the proliferation of information, which brings us so many advantages, which also makes a sales professional's job more difficult as customers are better educated and increasingly demanding. Many companies are taking advantage of this new information age by conducting reverse auctions where suppliers are invited to bid electronically on business. In many cases, these auctions are blind, with the bidder not even knowing the identity of the customer they're trying to acquire. In this case, price becomes the key and sometimes only differentiator.

One trend we continually see is supply chain optimization as a major corporate initiative and is bringing sales reps some unique new challenges. As an example, the purchasing department is growing in importance, as is its leadership. Many companies have elevated its top purchasing executives to a C-level title, Chief Procurement Officer. These CPOs are making it their mission to more closely manage their suppliers, eliminating value wherever possible.

Lastly, a trend some of our clients are experiencing are buying consortiums. These exist when different companies, often with little or nothing in common, come together solely to pool their buying power and use this growing leverage to drive down supplier prices.

Wright
Dan, what are the issues and challenges that sales professionals are dealing with because of these trends?

Kosch

Each of these trends create some difficult issues for us as we sell, especially if we're trying to sell value. I'd like to reflect on some of the issues that we're seeing out in the marketplace.

Competitive differentiation – the odds are people are finding it more and more difficult to differentiate themselves from their competitors. Everything looks the same to customers - especially to the procurement department!

Length and complexity of selling cycles - the length and complexity has increased dramatically. A lot of this is due to how many people, especially evaluators, can insert themselves into the selling process.

Changes in customer's organizations - with all the customer consolidations, (mergers and acquisitions), organizations are changing all the time; and the contacts that sales people call on are changing all the time.

Gaining and maintaining access to senior level decision makers - it's more challenging than ever for sales people as they are being blocked by gatekeepers like procurement or purchasing consultants, more now than ever before.

Being proactive rather than reactive – as an example, this means not waiting until there is an RFP to position your company as a resource to your customer. This is proving to be really challenging, especially if we've waited to follow a predetermined buying process.

Selling value versus price - you stand a low chance of being successful here if your only access is through the procurement process or if you're stuck responding to an internet auction. It's hard to position value if you're competing in an environment where the priority is placed on getting the best price.

Mark and I heard an executive say something interesting recently when reflecting on some of these issues with his sales team. He said, "The pie is getting smaller and the knives are getting sharper." We thought that this perspective reflected really well the tough environment out there.

Wright

So what is the future of the sales profession?

Shonka

Well, in the next several years, the nature of the sales profession will change significantly, especially the role of direct sales. Right now, we're seeing sales channels changing. There is increasing emphasis on inside sales and indirect sales channels as companies look to increase their coverage while lowering their cost of sales. This can result in the elimination of many direct sales jobs, especially in the ranks of the traditional territory sales rep, while adding indirect sales jobs. As one client told us, they are taking away many of their rep's car keys and handing out more and more phone headsets.

With this trend and so many other forces working to take the value out of the sale, sales professionals who want to continue to develop their career in direct sales need to rethink the way they sell. It's clear that traditional ways of selling and traditional ideas of selling value, or consultative selling, aren't enough anymore. Clearly, the bar has been raised. So sales professionals now have an obvious choice. They can do nothing or they can literally change the way they sell. As Max Depree has said, "We cannot become what we need to be by remaining what we are." In the future, for sales professionals who want to protect and develop their sales careers, they have to take their skills to new levels. They will either sell value or become a commodity, or as one client recently told us, they have to "sell value or die."

Wright

Dan, he said "sell value or become a commodity." What do you guys mean by that?

Kosch

As we think about that statement, "sell value or become a commodity," we need to ask ourselves, "Do we sell low price or do we sell value?" As Michael Porter, renowned expert on competitive advantage, points out - there are two key sources of competitive advantage. One, we have the low cost position which gives us the ability to be a price leader; or two, we're highly differentiated. If we're differentiated, we have to sell value. So although it seems pretty straight forward, if you're not low price and you are differentiated, you need to position and sell that value or become a commodity and have the emphasis of the decisions your customers make be based predominantly on price.

We recognize that this isn't easy. The trends and the issues that we've reflected on cause what we call the "value selling challenge." A) It's tougher to sell value than ever before. B) There are fewer people who can buy value. C) The people who buy value tend to be located higher in the organization. So in the end, if we don't sell value, the trends and issues will force us to be commoditized.

What can we start to do once we admit, "yes, we compete on value." First, selling value starts with our mindset. We have to assume an attitude, "I sell value." "I deserve to sell at senior levels." "I help my customers achieve their business objectives and address their business issues." A client of ours that did just this was a petroleum company. They sell grease—grease in cans and grease in barrels. But what happens if you sell grease, especially if you sell grease to people who buy grease? You'll become commoditized. In this case, the President, the VP of Sales and the entire sales organization had to first convince themselves that they didn't sell grease, but rather they sold solutions that included grease that would help plants run more effectively, drive more revenue, cut costs and improve quality. And that's exactly what they did. So it starts with our mindset!

Next, we have to believe that we need to and can go beyond just the traditional sources of competitive differentiation (service and product excellence, operational excellence or industry reputation.) We so often compete on those merits. We need to believe that how we sell or how we do business can actually be a key differentiator and help us elevate ourselves as we sell value.

Furthermore, we need to ask ourselves—what is the customer's perception of our value? Are we a *vendor* where the emphasis is on price and our relationships tend to be at low levels? Are we a *problem solver* where we are perceived as doing a really good job meeting the needs the customer has with our products and services? Are we a *business or a strategic resource* where we're looked at as making an impact within their business and our relationships are at all levels including senior levels?

We believe that what we do as we're selling and managing relationships has a lot to do with that perception and the results that come from that perception. We see a few key "selling value imperatives." 1) Selling value is a mindset, an approach, a set of strategies, and it is a process. 2) It is a realization that there is minimal value in product alone. 3) Selling value is positioning the value of our company and our solution above products and price. 4) It's recognition that there's no choice—we have to sell higher. 5) It's not following the customer's buying rules. 6) It's not an option, and it certainly isn't *trying* to sell value. It is selling value! Or we risk the chance of becoming a commodity.

Wright

So, Mark, what does the sales professional need to do to be successful in selling value in this tough environment?

Shonka

There are three key strategies that we believe sales people need to implement. First, it isn't enough to understand your customer's needs. You have to understand their business. Second, you can only sell value to people who can buy value. And third, it isn't enough to get to senior level management. You have to be so good you get invited back. To most experienced sales professionals, these three key strategies are obvious and even indisputable. Most sales professionals want to live these three strategies in their every day sales life. But this is tough because actually making changes in day to day behavior challenges all of us. Think about sales professionals. They are increasingly challenged in so many ways. They have rapidly changing markets. They have higher quotas. They're under more pressure for reporting and communication. And when challenged, sales professionals, like so many other people, fall back to instincts and actions that were more appropriate in the past. To prevent this, we recommend implementing a sales process to help live these three key strategies every day.

Wright

So what is the process you recommend for selling value?

Kosch

As we discussed earlier, we do believe that selling value starts with rethinking our mindset and then, as Mark points out, using a set of strategies. While those are important, it's hard to implement those things. So we *do* need a process for selling value and we *do* recommend a specific, strategic yet practical process for selling value. We call it the IMPAX® Process. It is a process that is laid out in our book, *Beyond Selling Value*. It's a process our company has worked with thousands and thousands of sales reps and managers to use - driving millions and millions of dollars of incremental revenue and associated profits.

At a high level, the process is a research driven, customer focused selling process that has three primary steps: first, research; second, communication; and third, presentation.

Research is all about understanding the customer's business from their perspective. It's about quickly getting a public perspective through data and an insider's perspective by conducting powerful research meetings or calls where we're asking insightful questions and doing a lot of listening.

The second step in the process, communication, is really about leveraging the knowledge we've gained in our research to gain access to senior level decision makers while at the same time dealing effectively with evaluators and potential gatekeepers.

And the third step of the process, presentation, is really all about making the most of an opportunity that we have with a senior level decision maker. It's about delivering a formal business presentation that focuses on the customer's business and then positions our company as a resource to help our customer achieve their objectives, implement their strategies, and address the issues that are most important to them.

The good news is that the IMPAX Process can be and is used in many different selling situations including: 1) large strategic and global accounts or small territory accounts, 2) new customer acquisition or closing opportunities at current customers, 3) closing deals or positioning a business relationship at a high level, 4) competitive or non competitive situations, 5) RFP or pre-RFP, 6) in North America or globally, 7) within the corporate environment or within the public sector, and 8) within any industry and with any set of products or services.

The last thought I might share here is one that came from an executive of D&B who described the process this way. He said, "The IMPAX Process is synonymous with customer focused selling. That's why customers are so receptive to doing business with us."

Wright

So why is research so important?

Shonka

Well, David, to answer that question let's go back to strategy number one. It isn't enough to understand your customer's needs. You have to understand your customer's business. Why is this true? Well, a key foundational belief of ours is this: that senior level decision makers are more likely to buy from us or partner with us because of what we know about them and their business than because of what they know about us and our products. Another way to think about this—lower level evaluators want to learn more about us, our products, and our company; but senior level decision makers only want to learn more about their own business and how they can improve it. Given that, let's take a look at three key benefits that research offers sales professionals.

First, credibility – time and again sales professionals using the process that Dan just referenced have leveraged the quality and depth of their research to blow away senior level decision makers. You know your research has paid off when the target of your presentation, a senior level executive, responds by saying, "You know more about our business than most of the people who work here." Good research also gives you a level of credibility in the decision maker's eyes that will prove crucial when you propose a strong business relationship with that customer's organization.

Second, professionalism – effective applied research is also key to elevating your own level of professionalism. High achieving sales people know more about their customers than mere product issues. They do research to improve their understanding of a customer's entire business from the customer's perspective. They become empowered to make recommendations that extend beyond the limited range of a product solution. In the decision maker's eyes, these sales people become true business resources, the kind who stand out from the throngs of venders trying to cram more products into an already overcrowded marketplace.

Third, distinction from the competition – today the differences among competing products have shrunk to the point where they are almost indistinguishable to many buyers. This is particularly true with senior level executives who tend to focus more on long term strategic issues than side by side product comparisons. By doing research, you set yourself apart from the competition, not by what you sell but by the way you sell and how well you understand your customer's business.

To make this a little clearer, I'd like to quote one of our clients, Martha Richardson, Director of Sales with Verifone, who shared her perspective on the research process. "I thought that my team and I were selling value, but I realized that we weren't. We weren't doing the right kind of research. We were focused on our solutions and requirements, but that's not selling value. Truly selling value means doing research about the customer's business so that we can position the business value associated with our relationship. The type of research we do now helps differentiate us from our competition."

Wright

So how do you recommend sales people efficiently conduct research?

Kosch

First, sales people need to know what they're looking for as they set out to do research, especially if they are selling value. Traditionally, sales people might have thought that the type of discovery they needed to do was either qualifying or application research. Qualifying research focuses on questions that help us understand if we have an opportunity worth pursuing. Application research focuses on questions that try to uncover the needs or application requirements that help us understand how our products and services will fit those needs. No doubt, we still need to be asking those types of questions, but today we must go beyond those traditional and more cursory areas of research. This is really important if we're selling value. We need to view selling value through a much larger lens focused on the customer's business versus a more traditional and limited lens focused on needs analysis. We had a software sales executive tell us what he thought about this. He said, "IMPAX is earning the business by learning the business."

So what are we looking for? We categorize the areas of research into what we call the IMPAXsearch™ elements. There are four key elements or "buckets" of knowledge that we want to gain.

1) **Corporate Profile and Direction**. Corporate profile includes things like the customer's products and services, their customers, their markets and their financials. Corporate direction includes the company's business objectives, their strategies, and their issues.

2) **Organizational Structure**. Here we want to make sure we understand not only the formal organization, but also the informal organization - knowing where the influence is within the company.

3) **Key Players and Profiles**. This area focuses on knowing the right things about the people in key buying roles. Examples of things you might want to learn are their professional background, their issues and concerns, their priorities, and their management style.

4) **Departmental Profile and Direction**. This area considers things similar to corporate profile and direction, but for the key departments that we're selling into such as sales, marketing, engineering, human resources, or information technology.

I mentioned that there are four elements, but there's really a fifth IMPAXsearch element. We call this "business fit." Based on what we

187

have learned in the first four IMPAXsearch elements, we want to develop a strategic business fit between our two companies.

Once we clearly know what we're looking for, we need to think about how we get that knowledge quickly and efficiently. There are two primary ways to do that. One is to get the "public perspective" or what we call data; and two, is to get the "insider perspective," or what we call information. The public perspective or data are the publicly available facts and figures about a company. We all can think of examples of data sources like annual and quarterly corporate reports, 10K reports, D&B information reports, articles, brochures, analyst reports, and of course, company websites. We can get these types of data sources in so many ways including the internet, calling the company, or asking our coaches. The thing that we have to remember though in getting data is that "getting data is administrative, using it is strategic." If we know what we're looking for, we can use it to help ask better questions in our research meetings and to help develop our business presentations to senior level decision makers.

Next is the insider perspective or what we call information. This is the unique insider perspective we get from conducting what are known as "research meetings" with people with insight on a customer's business. The research meeting is a distinct type of meeting where the focus is on improving our understanding of the customer's or prospect's business. It's not a product focused sales call. It's where we put to use what we call the 95-5 rule and move beyond data to gain a real insider's perspective. The 95-5 rule is when you listen 95% of the time and you talk 5%. When you're talking you're just asking better questions.

Research meetings can be done in person or they can be done over the phone. How long they last is really up to you and the person you are calling on. How many you do really depends on things like the opportunity potential or the time you have. The focus in these research meetings goes beyond those qualifying and more traditional application questions. You should be using your best questioning techniques to gain insight in the four IMPAXsearch elements that I just talked about. Example questions you might ask include: What are your company's business objectives for the coming year? What are your critical success factors? How will the business be different two years from now?

There's a sales executive that we work with, Tom Mezera, who is the Senior Vice President of Sales and Marketing Operations for a large financial outsourcing company. He believes strongly in research meetings. He reflected on research meetings by saying, "We want our sales process to be part of our competitive advantage. It's hard to do that if the questions we're asking are focused only on our solution fits. We needed to take an approach to questioning that took us to the next level—one that truly demonstrated our interest in our customer's business." So there are some clear ways to efficiently do research: know what you're looking for—the IMPAXsearch elements; get data through publicly available data sources; and get information through research meetings or calls.

Wright

So, Mark, what is the business fit and how is it different from the product fit?

Shonka

David, to answer this question; let's start by talking about product fit first. Every sales professional out there understands product fit. We've all been trained to understand our customer's needs or applications, and to relate our products or solutions to their situation. Product fit typically focuses on users and user management. It solves a specific departmental need. Often, product fit solves a short term problem and as a result, the customer's focus can quickly center on our products and our price. Some common product fit statements that many of us have used in the past might include these: "Our solution provides quick turnaround." "It enables increased throughput." "We can provide for smooth implementation." "We provide service after the sale."

But business fit is different. Business fit is how the two companies working together can help the customer achieve critical objectives, implement important strategies, and address key issues. It's longer term in nature, and it focuses on senior level management's business priorities. As a result, the focus is on value, which is measured in the customer's terms. Some common business fit statements, which are different than the product fit statements, could include these: "Working together, our relationship enhances attainment of your critical business objectives." "Our relationship builds on a set of common values." "Together we could strengthen your competitive advantage." "Our relationship results in a win-win partnership."

The real power of business fit is with senior level decision makers. These are the people who lie awake in bed at night worried about improving their business. When we do our research and can relate the

189

fit to them in business terms versus product terms, we can take their perception of us and our overall relationship to a whole new level.

A good way to bring this to light is to share an example of business fit in the real world. In this case study situation, we were working with a Dupont Agricultural Chemicals organization, and a rep specifically selling to a large grain company. He had been taught how to sell products and he's learned very well the key product characteristics that will drive product fit for him with his typical customers. But he knows in this situation that that's not enough, and he followed the process that we've laid out here so far in this discussion. In fact, he followed the process to a "T" and found himself with an opportunity to present to the President of the grain company. But his comment was, "What do I sell to the President of the grain company? It has to be different than what I sell a buyer of agricultural chemicals." Of course, he was right. He was trained to really hone in on some product characteristics to help make a sale. For instance, in this situation, the granular nature of his product would be a significant advantage over a liquid formulation that they were currently buying from a competitor. However, this rep realized that the President of the grain company didn't really care about granularity. But the President did have a key issue that could keep him awake at night. That issue was providing just in time delivery of chemicals to his farmer customers so that they increase yields, which in turn helps the grain company when they go to broker the farmer's grain. That's his number one issue, and this sales professional realized that the granularity feature can help the customer because it can help facilitate transportation and distribution to get customers what they need quickly. But he didn't want to share it in product fit terms. The term "granularity" would mean nothing to the President. So instead of focusing on what he was always taught to focus on, granularity, he simply shifted a little bit and focused on showing the President of the company how, working with DuPont, he could take this issue off his plate. He can truly move to just in time deliveries of critical chemicals to customers. That's what the President wanted and that's what the President bought. This example really drives out the difference between product fit and business fit.

There's a quote that also might provide a good conclusion to this question. This quote is by one of our clients, Errol Schoenfish, with Microsoft Business Solutions. He said, "Business fit really is different. For years sales people have been trying to get to the senior level decision makers, but when we got there we were underwhelming.

Business fit has given us a tool to show decision makers how we can help them resolve critical issues and attain objectives. They can now see us as a business resource, not just a product vendor."

Wright

It seems that getting to senior level decision makers is critical but difficult. How should sales people actually do this?

Kosch

As we think about actually getting to senior level decision makers, we're really talking about the second strategy that Mark discussed earlier, which is "you can only sell value to those who can buy it." In this strategy, we should be asking ourselves two questions in gaining access. First, who should we gain access to; and second, how should we gain access?

First, although it seems pretty straight forward, we should define the 'who' as the individual that we call the decision maker. A decision maker is really someone in the customer's or prospect's organization who can say "yes" to a decision even if everyone else says "no". Or they can say "no" and really mean it. They truly are the person you need to get to in order to sell your value. As we talked about earlier, they tend to be at more senior levels of the organization.

Once we know who we want to gain access to, we need to address "how." The best access strategy in any given situation is really the one with the highest odds of success and the lowest amount of effort. Our success here has a lot to do with the quality of our research and the quality of our coaches. Coaches are those individuals inside or outside the customer's organization that want us to win, and win if we win. They are willing to share insights with us and really "coach" us in executing our sales strategy at the account.

There are many different access strategies a sales rep can use. I'd like to list several and highlight three in particular. One access strategy is having the decision maker call us which is certainly the access strategy we all would love to use. Although this doesn't happen often, it does happen. When it does, we need to know how we are going to take advantage of it. Another access strategy is the event in the buying cycle, sometimes better known as "vendor day," where we have a chance to meet with the customer along with a number of other potential suppliers. There are other strategies such as coach introduction, a personal request, and writing an impactful, research oriented and customer focused access letter. It's these three strategies that I'd like to actually focus on. These can be very effective strategies as we try to gain access to decision makers.

First, the coach introduction is probably the most common strategy that is used. It's important that we find the right coach—one that's influential enough with the decision maker. It's also important that we "coach the coach" on how to position the request to the decision maker so that the odds are increased that we will be successful.

Secondly, there's the personal request. This is probably the most direct strategy. It's important that we consider if we have the relationship to gain access directly or if it would be better that our manager or someone else we know who does have the relationship and influence make the personal request. Whatever the case, it's important that we prepare and we know exactly how we're going to position our request. We would recommend that it not be a product focused request and a sales pitch, but rather it be a request that focuses on the "business fit" like Mark just highlighted. It should position how you believe that your company and you can be a resource to them and their organization.

The third strategy that I wanted to highlight is what we call the IMPAXaccess™ letter. This is a letter that focuses on our understanding of the customer's environment. It does not focus on us and our company and our products and services. It requests a business presentation meeting and doesn't try to sell us and our company. Although this strategy can be time consuming, it is very effective if we don't have a more efficient access strategy we can use.

In the end, there are many very powerful and proven ways to gain access to true decision makers. The important thing is to pick a strategy and get it done before you run into potential gatekeepers. We recommend that we all keep in mind Theodore Roosevelt's great quote and thoughts on decisiveness. He said, "In any moment of decision, the best thing you can do is the right thing. The next best thing you can do is the wrong thing. And the worst thing you can do is nothing." So in thinking about gaining access—know your situation, make a decision, and take action!

Wright

How do you suggest handling those gatekeepers that don't want you to get there?

Shonka

First of all, we have to decide to take on this challenge, and most sales professionals don't. Most sales professionals accept the block, believing that over time they'll be able to change their position through personality or persuasion. In this way, we become our own worst gatekeeper. One of our clients, a Senior Vice President of a high tech sales force, shared with us that about 90% of the time his sales force accepted the gatekeeper's block, and he was working very hard to help change that behavior. For those sales professionals who want to do it differently, we recommend a four step process for dealing with these gatekeepers.

The first step is to Assess the Risk and Opportunity. Ask yourself these two questions. What can I gain if I successfully convert or challenge the person who's blocking me? And second, what are the consequences if I challenge the person who's blocking me and I'm not successful? The answer to these questions will help determine how far you go with this opportunity. One way to easily arrive at this conclusion is to put together a simple T chart, a Ben Franklin diagram, if you will, with the pros and cons of the opportunity. Some of the pluses may include winning the business, bonuses, compensation, recognition, and future opportunities for cross selling. Some of the negatives might include making the gatekeeper mad, losing related business, or damage to your reputation. In looking at it in this way, it's easier to come to a conclusion in each situation.

If the pros outweigh the cons, it's time to move to step two, which is Understanding the Gatekeeper's Motivation. There are many different reasons why your gatekeeper may be blocking you. They may not want to lose control. They may feel threatened by your efforts. They may prefer the status quo. Or they may be your competitor's coach and simply want you to lose.

The answer to this question can help immensely as we consider step three, which is Consider Alternative Strategies. And there are many strategies to consider, both direct and indirect, which can be successful in different situations. These strategies include transforming the gatekeeper into a coach, involving the gatekeeper in the process, neutralizing the gatekeeper, leveraging your coaches, side-stepping the block, winning in another area, utilizing someone else in your company to drive above the gatekeeper to the decision maker, or going around the gatekeeper to the decision maker yourself.

In any case, step four is critical. We need to Select and Execute the Right Strategy. Brainstorming, getting other people's perspective, considering the "what ifs", and developing a fall back strategy are all part of professionally and proactively selecting and executing the right way. And as we consider this four step process, keep in mind the words of Wayne Gretzky. He said, "I miss 100% of the shots I never take." If we're selling value, we have to take our shots. We can't be our own gatekeeper, and we can't let gatekeepers stand between us and getting to C-level decision makers who can buy our value.

Wright

So, Dan, let me ask you a question about the third strategy, and that is, "It isn't enough to get to senior management. You've got to be so good that you get invited back." How do you guys accomplish this?

Kosch

Your question is an interesting one. It really asks, what is it that we can do when we have successfully gained access to the decision maker to be so compelling that we (one) not only establish a business relationship or close the business, but that (two) we come across with the credibility that earns us the right to access again and again in the future. No doubt this is quite a challenge, but one that we see clients handling every day.

In general, we need to do three things to be successful and to get invited back. First, we need to talk the customer's business. Second, we need to prove the business fit or the business value. And third, we need to communicate through a powerful business presentation. There are two underlying premises or guidelines that impact what we do here. Mark mentioned the first one earlier - the idea that senior level management is more likely to buy from or form a partnership with us based upon what we know about them and their business versus what they know about us and our products. The second premise is important here as well - for effective positioning, the power of a presentation exceeds the power of just a product demonstration or a discussion.

There are many reasons why we should make a business presentation. For instance, it helps us establish the basis for a business relationship. It can differentiate us from competition. It helps create a decisive environment. It helps us create an impression of professionalism. It also helps us create the right perception of our company as a business resource and not a product vendor. And no doubt, it also assists us in directing the meeting with the decision maker so it doesn't get off track. And there are many more that we could add to that list. As a matter of fact, there was an interesting study done at the University of Minnesota that concluded that if you stand up and give a presentation, that (one) your customer is 43% more likely to be persuaded and (two) they'll be willing to pay 26% more money for the same product or service. This certainly helps justify why we should stand up and present.

So, if we agree that we should stand up and present, the question becomes, "What is it we should present?" What we do know is what we should not do, and that is to use the traditional approach and make a product presentation or product pitch, which one of our clients called the "old show up and throw up" presentation - everything you wanted to know about us but were afraid to ask! That certainly is what we don't want to do. Our recommendation is that your business presentation include a number of key elements to be impactful. One, you start with a cover page that's entitled *A Business Presentation*. The customer's logo is front and center. You certainly have a page on the presentation objectives. You have a page on the agenda. And then you get to the section of the presentation that often is not done, and that's the customer's business where you address your understanding of their business objectives, their business strategies, their business issues, and your understanding of their key departmental issues. Then you move to your company's business. You highlight the business fit, and then if applicable, you would talk about your solution and solution fit. And finally conclude with recommendations, action steps, and a time table.

It's important as we think about those elements that we think about how we deliver the customer section in particular. It needs to be delivered in a humble, more confirming tone as opposed to a confident, informing tone that we might use in delivering the section on our company.

So if you follow this approach, the presentation you make will be different and it will make you different – and that's a good thing! Use your presentation to differentiate yourself based not just on what you sell, but how you sell it, especially if you're selling value and selling to senior level management.

Wright

Well, we've covered a lot of important topics, important to me. I'm going to use some of these things, think about them, and I may even write you or e-mail you and get some more answers to some more questions. But before we leave, I think I'd like to give either or both of you the opportunity to wrap up anything that I might not have covered in my questions that you think would benefit the readers and listeners of these conversations on customer service and sales.

Shonka

You know, David, we've covered an awful lot of ground so let's draw a quick conclusion. We'd say that in an increasingly challenging sales environment, direct sales professionals who want to make sales their career long term have to change. They have to take their skills to the next level. We talked about three key strategies to help make this happen. First, it isn't enough to understand your customer's needs; you have to understand their business. Second, you can only sell value to people who can buy it. And third, it isn't enough to get to senior level management; you have to be so good you get invited back. But it's not enough to recognize or even agree with these three key strategies. We have to change our day to day sales activities, and we recommended the IMPAX sales process as a way to make this happen. The key steps of the process as we've laid it out today are first, do your research to develop that critical understanding of your customer's business. Second, leverage this research to communicate effectively in order to gain access to senior level decision makers who can buy your value, and deal with gatekeepers effectively who want to keep you from getting there. And third, present to your senior level decision makers in an effective and compelling way by focusing first on your customer and emphasizing the business fit between you and the customer. By using this process, you really can elevate the customer's perception of you as a business resource, thus differentiating you and your company from your competition. In this day and age this is more critical than ever before. You can learn so much more about this process in our best selling sales book, *Beyond Selling Value, a Proven Process to Avoid the Vendor Trap,* published by Dearborn and available on amazon.com and on our own website www.impaxcorp.com.

Kosch

As Mark summarizes, the thing I'd add is that - in the end - the process works! Get out, use it! We have seen so many results over the years. Results that lead to increased sales and more profitable business. We see companies changing the perception of themselves in the marketplace, and sales reps changing their customer's perceptions of them from a "vendor" to a "business resource." The process works! We'd love to hear from you about your success stories.

Wright

Today we've been talking to Mark Shonka and Dan Kosch. They are co-authors of *Beyond Selling Value,* and Co-Presidents of IMPAX Corporation. Both are highly sought after authorities on a range of sales topics as you have found out today. More importantly they're very highly thought of and sought after as speakers, trainers, and consultants. Guys, I really do appreciate the time that both of you have taken. I have really learned a lot and I'm sure our readers and our listeners will. Thank you so much for taking this much time to be with me and answering all of these questions on *Conversations on Customer Service and Sales.*

About The Authors

Co-authors and IMPAX Corporation Co-Presidents Mark Shonka and Dan Kosch have tallied more than 45 years of experience in direct sales, sales management, and sales consulting and training. IMPAX, a leading sales performance improvement company, is committed to helping clients improve their sales, account management, and sales leadership efforts to drive business results. IMPAX has worked with thousands of sales professionals in the field and the classroom throughout North America and abroad.

Shonka and Kosch are highly sought-after authorities on a range of sales topics including selling value, strategic account selling, strategic account management, and sales leadership. With names like IBM, 3M, DuPont, Eli Lilly, D&B, AT&T, and Microsoft, the authors' client list reflects some of the world's leading sales organizations. The authors wish to acknowledge Dave Matlow, who created the IMPAX process and is the founder of IMPAX Corporation. If you would like more information about IMPAX and about how we can help your company go Beyond Selling Value, please contact us at:

Mark Shonka & Dan Kosch

IMPAX

61 Wilton Road

Westport, Connecticut 06880-1908

Toll free: 800.457.4727

Office: 203.222.1900

Fax: 203-222.8445

E-mail: info@impaxcorp.com

www.impaxcorp.com

Chapter 12

RICHARD TYLER

THE INTERVIEW

David E. Wright (Wright)

Today we are talking to Richard Tyler. Richard is the CEO of Richard Tyler International, Inc., an organization that is one of the top training and consulting firms in the world. Mr. Tyler's success in sales, management, leadership, customer service, and quality improvement, and his reputation for powerful educational methods and motivational techniques have made him one of the most sought after consultants, lecturers, and teachers. Mr. Tyler shares his philosophies with millions of individuals each year through keynote speaking, syndicated writing, radio, television, seminars, books, tapes, and CDs. Mr. Tyler's book, *Smart Business Strategies, the Guide to Small Business Marketing Excellence,* has been hailed as one of the best books ever written for small business marketing. His *Power Learning Series* of business books and his *Conversations On* books are a great success. His philosophies have been featured in *Entrepreneur Magazine* and *Sales and Marketing Management Magazine* as well as in hundreds of articles and interviews. Mr. Tyler is the founder of Leadership for Tomorrow™, an organization dedicated to educating young adults to the importance of self esteem, goal setting, and lifelong success. Mr. Tyler is a member of the *National*

Speakers Association, the *International Platform Association*, the *American Society for Training and Development*, and the *Society for Human Resource Management*. Mr. Tyler has served on the *Houston National Speakers Association* Board of Directors. For 14 consecutive years Mr. Tyler has been listed in Who's Who in Professional Speaking. Mr. Tyler is an Advisory Board Member and past Chairman of the *"Be An Angel Fund, Inc."* which helps multiply handicapped and profoundly deaf children to have a better life.

Richard Tyler, welcome to *Conversations on Customer Service and Sales.*

Richard Tyler (Tyler)

Thank you, David. It is a pleasure to be here today.

Wright

Richard you are the CEO of a highly respected international consulting and training firm; how critical would you say customer service has been to the sales success of your business?

Tyler

On a scale of 1 to 10, I'd have to say 12. Without hesitation, I can tell you that excellent customer service is the single most important reason Richard Tyler International is successful. Yet, even with all the attention we give customer service, we're still working hard every day to improve our performance.

If you look at two companies that compete in the same market for the same customer and one is much more successful than the other, I guarantee the successful one provides better customer service. The impact of customer service is just that obvious.

Wright

So, if it's that important, and the impact that obvious, are companies generally providing good customer service?

Tyler

Unfortunately, yes; and therein lies the problem. Too many companies are comfortable simply providing "good" customer service. Customers *expect* good customer service. So when they get it, there is nothing that tells the customer that this company is different than any other.

What impresses customers—what they really want—is *Excellent* customer service. And in my experience, it is Excellent customer service that is rare. When customers experience it, they not only appreciate it, they reward the companies that provide it with increased loyalty.

Wright

What does Excellent customer service look like in a sales organization?

Tyler

It's not one thing. In fact, I'd say it's *everything*. People hear me say it a lot, but I believe Excellence is an attitude, a commitment to accept nothing less than the very best, no matter how difficult, no matter how uncomfortable, no matter how stressful. It's never easy to achieve, and when it <u>describes</u> an entire sales organization, it's because it <u>involves</u> the entire sales organization. From the receptionist to the shipping clerk to the sales manager to the CEO—the entire organization recognizes that it takes a concerted effort to understand the customer and the customer's wants and needs well enough to be able to consistently provide Excellent customer service.

Wright

For a sales organization that wants to be known for providing excellent customer service, what would you say is the first step?

Tyler

There is no question that the starting place is to understand the customer. Most people will tell you they believe they understand their customer. But those companies that provide Excellent customer service make understanding the customer a relentless pursuit. They never assume they know their customer. Rather, they have systems in place to constantly evaluate their customers' wants and needs. It's that pursuit that begins creating an attitude of Excellent customer service.

Wright

Certainly every organization *wants* to be known for Excellent customer service; what prevents them from doing so?

Tyler

One of the biggest hurdles is functional independence. I've worked with many organizations over the years, and I often see a great number of independent functions loosely cobbled together. The different components of the organization—research and development, engineering, sales, distribution, etc.—work independently from one another with only the minimum amount of necessary communication. This independence creates a separation and often fosters animosity as well as individual and group power structures.

The Excellent sales organizations start with a commitment to Excellent customer service training for everyone in the company. Each employee has a genuine interest in how every other person serves the customer. Although it's not thought of as a sales organization, take a look at Southwest Airlines. Every employee is cross trained. One reason the company does it is to ensure that employees understand what other opportunities there are inside the company. But a result is that at any given time, a flight attendant can pitch in to help an overwhelmed gate agent; or a pilot who is riding as a passenger on a particular flight can lend a hand to the busy flight attendants.

Southwest's focus is always the customer and that's not only apparent to the customer, but to the investors as well. Southwest is one of the only airlines in the world that is consistently making a profit. I believe that has everything to do with their commitment to Excellent customer service.

Wright

Your company does quite a bit of international consulting. Do you see key differences in customer service among cultures?

Tyler

Of course, there are cultural differences in how people communicate, but it's my experience that the principles of Excellent customer service are universal. Regardless of where you are from or where you are living, I believe every person's investment decisions are motivated by a desire to gain pleasure or profit or by a desire to avoid pain or loss. I have yet to find a culture where this is not true—and since I believe this is human behavior; I doubt I'll find one.

Once you understand how to communicate appropriately in each culture, the strategy that underlies successful selling is universal. It's a matter of working to understand what factors are shaping the customer's motivation and finding ways your product or service can meet that customer's wants or needs. In our sales training programs, we spend quite a bit of time teaching ways to determine a customer's investment motives. This process helps a sales team better understand how its company's products or services can meet the customer's wants or needs. Again, this works regardless of culture.

Wright

Is providing that extraordinary level of customer service a skill anyone can develop or are some of us just born with it?

Tyler

That's an interesting question. You know, we are all customers of many companies, and we can all think of times when we received horrendous customer service as well as times when we received Excellent customer service. So, given that we know the difference between the two, you would think that providing Excellent customer service would come naturally.

Unfortunately, it's simply not that easy. I liken it to watching a professional golfer in action. The swing of the club looks effortless. And to someone who has never played golf, it really looks very easy. But for the first timer, there is nothing easy about it. There is so much involved with positioning your shoulders, arms, hands, knees and feet. And there's a real science to the arc of the swing, momentum, leverage and so on, that anyone who has done it understands there is nothing automatic about a good golf swing.

Just seeing Excellence in action doesn't necessarily teach us how to do it. Those who are really interested in developing a reputation for providing Excellent customer service must be committed to constant improvement, constant education and constant practice. Yes, I believe that everyone *can* learn, it just takes dedication and a long-term commitment.

Wright

You mentioned that understanding the customer's wants and needs is the first step on the road to establishing a reputation for excellent customer service. What are the next steps necessary to using customer service to set a sales organization apart from the competition?

Tyler

Focus on the first-contact environment. This is the first-impression stage of the customer interaction. If you want to turn that interaction into an advantage, you must focus on making the best-possible first impression. This is true no matter what you are selling.

What happens in the first 60 seconds of a customer's experience with your company sets the tone for the rest of the relationship. As a customer, that first experience is difficult to forget. If it's a good one, you may forgive a slip-up here or there. If the experience is a bad one, there's a good chance you'll be looking to someone else to satisfy your wants and needs.

The sales professional that provides Excellent customer service thinks through and plans every detail of the first impression and leaves nothing to chance. The reason this is so important is that customers make decisions about a company in the first 60-second exposure. And once that initial decision is made, the customer tends to search for evidence to support that first impression while dismissing information that conflicts with it.

The bottom line is that you simply cannot spend too much time preparing for that first impression.

Wright

What advice would you give to the sales person who wants to establish a reputation for providing excellent customer service, but doesn't work in an organization that provides the necessary support?

Tyler

This is unfortunately a very common dilemma for many fine sales professionals who are committed to Excellence. The first option of course is to simply leave and find an organization that *does* support this goal. This should be a realistic consideration given that the company may never appreciate and embrace the concept. The reality is that if the company is not committed to providing Excellent customer service today, it most likely will not be tomorrow. But there is always hope, and there are certainly things the sales professional can do.

First, recognize and acknowledge that you *do* have control over some things. Perhaps it is your time, your prospecting strategies, your presentation format, etc. Then, focus your energy on improving each of those components. Seize every training opportunity you can—even if it means paying for it on your own. Good training programs are usually worth many times their investment. A hallmark of every sales professional I know who provides Excellent customer service is the commitment to development.

Many people mistakenly believe that the Excellent sales professional simply has a natural gift that requires little development. Although I agree that some people can have certain natural talents relevant to the sales business, my experience has been that to be great—to be known for providing Excellent customer service, you have to sharpen the tools all the time. I frequently tell sales professionals that if they want to see continuous improvement in their skills and in their results, they must make it a habit to regularly evaluate their current abilities, and at least quarterly identify some type of training and development they will complete to improve those abilities. Consistently taking this step alone will put that sales professional in the top 10% of all salespeople.

Wright

Based on your experience in training thousands of sales professionals, what is one of the first training programs you would recommend to someone committed to developing a reputation for customer service Excellence?

Tyler

Regardless of the sales professional's level of experience; I would recommend a course on the fundamentals of selling. I know that may sound surprising—especially if we're talking about experienced salespeople. But it's the fundamentals that are often most overlooked. When fundamental skills get rusty, performance suffers, regardless of how long a person has been selling.

We teach a series of sales education courses as Immersion Programs™. Each program is very intense. The participants are engaged for up to 15 hours a day focused on fine-tuning their skills. Our most popular Sales Immersion Program™ is the initial program in the series that focuses on fundamentals. The surprising fact to some is that the average participant has more than ten years of professional sales experience. We often see extremely successful sales professionals come through this course. They understand that you can never focus too much on the fundamentals. That's what commitment to Excellence is all about. Some of our participants return to the program many times. They consider this program their version of professional sports pre-season training—the opportunity to re-sharpen the tools and strengthen those skills that are already strong.

Wright

I have heard that sales professionals who lose customers often never know why the customer stopped doing business with them. Is this a reflection of poor customer service?

Tyler

Many times, yes. But it is more a reflection of the salesperson's inability to create the correct rapport with the customer.

It is true that sales professionals often never discover why customers stop doing business with them. In fact, research suggests that 75 of every 100 customers a company loses will never tell the company why they left for the competition. If the salesperson responsible for that account doesn't know why the customer left, it's usually because he or she did not ask.

This can become a big problem if the salesperson is doing something—or not doing something—that is driving the business away. If the salesperson doesn't learn what is causing the loss of customers, he or she has a high probability of continuing to make the same error.

Wright

So how does a sales professional improve his or her chances of getting feedback from the customer before it is too late?

Tyler

It starts with the fundamental skill of rapport-building. We teach a concept called "The Tyler 4"™ Fundamentals™. Although every business is unique, these fundamentals are universal. The very first of these fundamentals is rapport building. Building a solid rapport with the customer must begin with the first interaction, and continue throughout the relationship. This not only sets the appropriate stage for learning the customer's true Wants and Needs™, but it creates a relationship that helps keep communications open when something is not going well.

The sales professional committed to customer service Excellence understands this and regularly asks for feedback from the customer about what is going well and what is not going well. With this discipline in place, it is rare for sales people or their companies to be blindsided by the customer's decision to stop doing business.

This seemingly simple process consistently practiced *will* separate the good from the Excellent. And as a result, the sales professional will lose fewer customers, and the Excellent customer service will earn additional business.

Wright

In closing, what comments do you want to make about customer service and sales?

Tyler

In order to create and sustain success an individual and/or a company must remember that sales and service are linked together. Customer service is a part of the sales process, for that reason all service personnel need to be thoroughly educated in fundamental sales processes.

From a customer's perspective; for the customer to perceive the sales experience as excellent they must receive excellent service and for the customer to perceive the service as excellent they must receive excellence in sales. What the customer is *really* investing in is the entire experience. Individuals and companies that understand this and use this concept as a point of positive differentiation train constantly to rigorous standards. The reward is always more satisfied, loyal customers. And satisfied loyal customers, invest in more products and services, they are less expensive to keep than a new customer is to attract and they refer new customers which lowers the acquisition costs of those new customers. As a result the investments made by an individual or company in training and education are easily recovered and eclipsed by the higher profitability associated with satisfied, loyal customers.

The bottom line of all this is; companies must invest in on going sales training for all their people from the front line to the front desk if they want to create an Excellent Sales and Service experience and reap the rewards. Individual sales and service people should do the same even if their company is providing training and must do the same if their company isn't providing training.

I guarantee every company and individual doing this is on their way to enjoying market dominance.

Wright

It is always a pleasure to talk with you, Richard. Today we've been talking to Richard Tyler. Richard is the CEO of Richard Tyler International, an organization that's one of the top training and consulting firms in the world. Thank you for taking this time to share your insights on customer service and sales.

Tyler

Thank you, David.

About The Author

Richard Tyler is the CEO of **Richard Tyler International, Inc.™** an organization named one of the top training and consulting firms in the world. Mr. Tyler's success in sales, management, leadership, quality improvement and customer service and his reputation for powerful educational methods and motivational techniques, has made him one of the most sought after consultants, lecturers, teachers and success coaches. Mr. Tyler shares his philosophies with millions of individuals each year through keynote speaking, syndicated writing, radio, television, seminars, books, compact discs and tapes.

Mr. Tyler's book *SMART BUSINESS STRATEGIES™, The Guide to Small Business Marketing EXCELLENCE* has been hailed as one of the best books ever written for small-business marketing. His successful books include; *Leadership Defined, Real World Customer Service Strategies That Work, Real World Human Resource Strategies That Work, Real World Teambuilding Strategies That Work, Conversations on Success, Conversations on Customer Service & Sales, Conversations on Health & Wellness, Conversations on Faith*, and *Marketing Magic*. His philosophies have been featured in *Entrepreneur Magazine®* as well as in hundreds of articles and interviews.

Mr. Tyler is the founder of the Leadership for Tomorrow™ an organization dedicated to educating young adults in the importance of self-esteem, goal setting and life-long success. He serves on the Advisory Board and is past Board Chairperson to Be An Angel Fund, a non-profit organization helping multiply handicapped children and profoundly deaf children to have a better life.

Richard Tyler

Richard Tyler International, Inc.™

P.O. BOX 630249

Houston, Texas 77263-0249

Phone: 713.974.7214

Email: RichardTyler@RichardTyler.com

WEBSITES

www.RichardTylerInternational.com

www.RichardTyler.com

www.SalesImmersion.biz

www.TylerTraining.com

www.ExcellenceEdge.com

www.DiscEducation.com

BOOK WEBSITES

www.LeadershipDefined.biz

www.ConversationsOn.biz

www.RealWorldStrategies.biz

www.MarketingMagicBook.biz